The Making of
THE LIVING
PLANET

London
GEORGE ALLEN & UNWIN in association with ABSOLUTE PRESS
Boston   Sydney

By   arrangement   with   the   BRITISH   BROADCASTING
CORPORATION

The Making of
THE LIVING
PLANET
Andrew Langley

George Allen & Unwin (Publishers) Ltd,
40 Museum Street, London WC1A 1LU, UK
in association with
Absolute Press (Publishers)
14 Widcombe Crescent, Bath BA2 6AH, UK

George Allen & Unwin (Publishers) Ltd,
Park Lane, Hemel Hempstead, Herts HP2 4TE, UK

George Allen & Unwin Australia Pty Ltd,
8 Napier Street, North Sydney, NSW 2060, Australia

First published in 1985

British Library Cataloguing in Publication Data

Langley, Andrew
    The making of the living planet.
1. Living planet (Television program)
I. Title
791.45'72   PN1992.77.L5
ISBN 0-04-778002-9

Book designed by Sue Aldworth

Set in 11 on 12½ point Garamond by
Mathematical Composition Setters Ltd, Salisbury, Wiltshire, UK
Colour reproduction by Scan Studios, Dublin
Printed in Great Britain by Hazell Watson and Viney Limited,
Member of the BPCC Group, Aylesbury, Bucks

FOREWORD

The English language has not yet evolved a universally accepted word to describe the person, male or female, who appears on a television screen alongside, behind, occasionally beneath and usually in front of, animals. Americans, perhaps a little effusively to English ears, call him or her a 'host'. British television tends to refer to him or her as the 'narrator' or 'presenter'. More jocularly, less flatteringly and maybe with a certain amount of justice, he is sometimes called in the trade a 'nature-jockey'. This uncertainty is hardly surprising for it is almost impossible for an innocent viewer to discover exactly what contribution this enigmatic character has made to the programme in which he appears. He may have been called in at the last moment and have little idea as to what has happened and will happen in the film when he is not visibly in it. He may not even be speaking his own words, but be reading those written by someone else held up in front of him on a board out of sight of the camera. On other occasions, both the thoughts and the words he expresses may be his own. He may even have played a part in the shaping of the programme as a whole.

But however much he may have done, it is none the less a rare presenter who truly deserves as much credit as he usually gets. His appearance in the film seems to lead many of those watching to identify him with every aspect of its production. Only too often he is assumed not only to have written every word heard, and conceived every sequence seen, but to have personally pressed the camera button and taken every shot of the film, not excluding those in which he himself appears.

The assumption is usually, of course, a subconscious one. A moment's thought is enough for anyone to realise that many other people must have been involved. The fact is that any danger the narrator is seen to be facing is also being faced equally by the cameraman, recordist and director – except that they have the added handicap of being laden and obstructed by technical equipment; and often the shot that is the high-spot of the film, that has clearly taken hours and hours of patient observation and an almost telepathic ability to anticipate an animal's actions, was taken by a cameraman working, watching and waiting, often in acutely uncomfortable conditions, all by himself.

So it is a true pleasure to welcome this book which – for one television series at least – makes it clear how very many people contributed to the finished product, how very considerable their contributions were, and that the clichés spoken by almost every award winner at every television and film festival describing how much he owes to others are, like most clichés, absolutely true.

David Attenborough

ACKNOWLEDGEMENTS

This book is very much a team effort. The author and publishers would like to thank the following people – both BBC staff members and freelance – for their contributions:

First and foremost, Richard Brock, the executive producer of the series, without whose initial enthusiasm and continuing encouragement the book would never have been written at all;

David Attenborough;

Producers Ned Kelly and Andrew Neal, assistant producers Ian Calvert, Richard Matthews and Adrian Warren, and the production staff of Nicola Holford, Beth Huntley, Diana Richards and Marney Shears;

Andrew Buchanan, the unit manager;

Rosi Crane, film librarian, and researchers John Waters, Keith Scholey and Cathy Mackenzie;

BBC cameramen Martin Saunders and Hugh Maynard, and sound recordist Lyndon 'Dicky' Bird;

Independent film-makers Hugh Miles, Neil Rettig and Stephen Bolwell, and the London Scientific team of Alasdair MacEwen, Martyn Colbeck and Tim Chard;

Andrew Naylor, David Barrett and Sue Outlaw in the cutting rooms;

Margaret Perry, who did the graphics, and Elizabeth Parker, who composed the music;

John Kelly of BBC Enterprises;

Pat Phillips who transcribed the tapes;

and all unnamed who gave a helping hand, wittingly or otherwise.

CONTENTS

PREFACE

In an English zoo in Norfolk, two men are having a hard time with a giant anteater. They have a film camera, a fibreglass tube and 200 termites and they are trying to persuade the anteater to flick its whip-like tongue down the tube and pick off a few termites for the benefit of the camera.

In a jungle in Costa Rica, two other men are having an even harder time with a length of rope. There is 300 feet of it, and they are attempting to stretch it between two giant trees at a height of 130 feet. Once this is done, one of them will slide out across the yawning gap attached to a pulley block, filming as he goes.

On an ice sheet in the Arctic Circle, another pair has attracted the close attention of a polar bear, which is advancing with its head down and its ears back, sensing easy prey. While one man continues to shoot film of the bear, the other fires a warning bullet over its head. At the last minute the huge creature is distracted by the appearance of a rival and lopes away to drive it off.

In a brightly lit studio in London's Camden Town, a cameraman is waiting patiently for a small freshwater fish to jump out of its tank and lay its eggs on a conveniently placed leaf. This is the fourth batch of this particular species of fish that he has managed to get hold of, but not one has yet performed in the required manner.

In a hide in Surinam, another cameraman sits in sweltering heat trying to film the elusive courting dance of the cock-of-the-rock bird. Grass lice are crawling up his shins and a breakfast of porridge lies heavily in his stomach, but he dare not move for fear of disturbing his quarry.

In a boat in the middle of the Indian Ocean an entire film crew is lost. The captain of the craft, which has been hired, reveals that he has only the skimpiest knowledge of navigation and cannot use a sextant. Their destination is the island of Aldabra, over 700 miles from civilisation.

On a remote Scottish hillside, a hot-air balloon has landed on top of a barbed wire fence. The basket has tipped over, depositing the pilot, cameraman, sound recordist and producer in a tangled heap. While they sort out their equipment, parachutes and oxygen masks, a fifth man walks down to a nearby farmhouse to telephone for assistance. He knocks on the back door and it is opened by the farmer, who after a moment's scrutiny says: 'You're that chap who does the programmes on television with the animals.' He shows little surprise. David Attenborough acknowledges the truth of this statement, and the farmer continues: 'Then you'd be knowing the Professor of Zoology at the University of Aberdeen?' As a matter of fact this too is true, and is admitted to. 'Then', concludes the farmer with an air of triumph, 'you'd be interested to learn that his wife was born in this very house!'

It is hardly surprising that David Attenborough should have been accepted so readily as part of the natural scenery, even if he did seem to have materialised from nowhere. None of those mentioned in the preceding vignettes is likely to have been recognised by even the most ardent and well-informed devotee of natural history film-making, but Attenborough has been a well-known figure on our television screens for more than three decades. Series such as *Zoo Quest, Eastwards with Attenborough, Life on Earth* and *The Living Planet* have shown him on location in an astonishing variety of lands, and he has told the stories of his adventures in several bestselling books. What has not been told before, however, is the story of that devoted band of people who made all these programmes possible – the producers, cameramen, sound recordists, editors and office staff who remained resolutely on the unglamorous side of the camera. This book is an attempt to tell that story as it concerned the making of *The Living Planet*. It has been written with the cheerful co-operation of those mentioned in the text (plus several who were not), and the author would like to thank them all for their friendly patience and helpfulness towards a mere outsider.

BIRTH OF A SERIES

One of the golden rules of the entertainment industry is that you stick to a winning formula. The extraordinary success of the two television series *Life on Earth* and *The Living Planet* can largely be attributed to the fact that they combined two winning formulae. The first of these was the traditional natural history film, which the BBC has been perfecting over more than 30 years, most notably through the work of its Natural History Unit in Bristol. Formally founded in 1957, the Unit has established a unique reputation throughout the world for its high standards of production, the integrity of its attitudes and the adventurous spirit of its projects. It has put before the public a steady steam of unforgettable wildlife programmes, filmed or presented by such remarkable men as Peter Scott, Gerald Durrell, Eric Ashby, Heinz Sielmann – and David Attenborough.

The public appetite for natural history films is apparently insatiable. Many of the reasons for this are obvious: animals and plants can be very beautiful; their behaviour can vary from the spectacular to the comic, from the ferocious to the lovable; in order to watch them the viewer may be transported to the most exotic of locations – places he would never dream of being able to visit in the flesh – and yet stay in the comfortable security of his armchair. The other reasons are less obvious. A wildlife film is a silent intrusion upon the privacy of the natural world, and gives the viewer the opportunity of spying on that world in the knowledge that none of the animals is performing especially for his benefit. Unselfconscious behaviour in

A classic sequence David Attenborough and friends in *Life on Earth* (*John Sparks*)

front of a camera is rare enough to be treasured. The remarkable sophistication of modern filming techniques, which allows us to peer into birds' nests and badger setts, and to watch every detail of the development of a caddis fly, has perhaps increased this sense of privileged insulation as it has increased knowledge. But in a largely urbanised society, the only way that most people come in contact with natural history is through their television screens; the enormous popularity of wildlife films show how important is even this second-hand contact.

The second formula upon which *Life on Earth* and *The Living Planet* were based was of rather more recent vintage. It was in 1969 that Kenneth Clark's series *Civilisation* was transmitted on BBC2 and carried all before it. The idea of a 12- or 13-part blockbuster, examining all aspects of a major topic and illustrating it with examples from all over the world, was new, as was the lavish scale upon which the series was conceived. *Civilisation* was an astounding success, and was followed by Jacob Bronowski's *Ascent of Man* and Alistair Cooke's *America*, each of which made a similar impact. Which subject should be considered next? It seemed clear to the producers in the Natural History Unit that it should be the world of nature, which presented boundless opportunities for magnificent visual effects. They, however, were in Bristol and the men who made the big decisions were in London, and television management was at that time not renowned for its indulgent attitude towards the Natural History Unit.

The necessary link was provided, appropriately enough, by David Attenborough. After two decades of being Britain's most glamorous populariser of natural history he had left the screen to work in management, becoming Controller of BBC2 and then Director of Programmes for all of BBC Television. He was even tipped to be appointed as the next Director General. This effectively prevented him from writing and presenting programmes of his own and, as the years went by, he became more restless in his desk-bound role. When Christopher Parsons, a long-serving member of the Natural History Unit, came to see him with suggestions for a 'mega-series' on the natural world he gave no firm commitment but, as Parsons later recalled: 'I thought I noticed a gleam in his eye.' That gleam grew into *Life on Earth*, which David Attenborough wrote and narrated after resigning from his post with the BBC.

Martin Saunders One of the *Life on Earth* cameramen (*John Sparks*)

Life on Earth was three years in the making, and was at that time the most ambitious project ever undertaken by the Unit – or by any other wildlife film-makers. When it went on the air in 1979, the reaction of the viewing public astonished even the BBC management. In Britain, the two weekly transmissions were watched by a total of 15 million people, and the Reaction Index (a measure out of 100 of the audience's appreciation of each programme) exceeded 90 – a figure rarely achieved by any previous natural history film. The series, co-produced with Warner Brothers, was sold to television networks throughout the world and was greeted with rapture wherever it was shown. David Attenborough's book, based on the series, sold over 3 million copies in Britain alone.

The combination of the two winning formulae – wildlife film and lavish blockbuster series – with the charm and palpable enthusiasm of David Attenborough was clearly worth repeating, and even before *Life on Earth* had been completed two people were piecing together their own ideas independently of each other. One was Attenborough himself, who had a special interest in geology, and felt this was a major element lacking from *Life on Earth*. The other was Richard Brock, a producer who had worked on the series and earlier programmes with Attenborough, and who had built up a good working relationship with him.

Brock's first sketch was tentatively entitled 'Man on Earth' and was based on the eccentric premise that a Martian ecologist travels through the sterility of space and discovers, to his amazement, the fertile planet Earth. This little green man, with concomitant 'think' balloons, would observe the effect that Man has had upon this planet

Richard Brock Who worked with David Attenborough on *Life on Earth*, and became executive producer of *The Living Planet* (AW)

over the centuries and make appropriately detached judgements. This study of the ecological impact of *Homo sapiens* would, Richard Brock felt, form a natural sequel to *Life on Earth* and could again be presented by David Attenborough. The idea was committed to paper and included with various other suggestions from the Natural History Unit in a list of new projects offered to the Controller of BBC2 Television. Almost as an afterthought, an alternative was added: by splitting up the Earth into, say, ten natural regions, a rather more ambitious series might show how Man has affected each one, draining marshes, harnessing river power, polluting oceans and so on. The Controller's reaction to this as yet nebulous proposal was blunt and non-committal: 'Probably one longish programme. The idea needs more work.'

Richard Brock gradually began to marshal his thoughts into a more coherent form. The Martian was the first casualty, not surprisingly (although the concept of the 'space-traveller's eye-view' of Earth survived into the final series with the use of a model of the planet to illustrate meteorological and other matters). Man himself took a back seat as Brock's attention focused on the different kinds of habitat in the world. The new working title was 'Wild Places', and the series was intended to concentrate on each region in turn – the rainforests of the Cameroon, for example, or the icy scenery of northern Alaska. It was still thought of as a relatively modest undertaking, consisting of half-a-dozen programmes presented – if he was willing – by David Attenborough.

At first Richard Brock hesitated about putting his proposals to Attenborough, feeling that he might not want to get embroiled in another mammoth enterprise so soon after completing *Life on Earth*. Quite the opposite was the case. David Attenborough was ready and willing to join in and to add his own ideas for a series, with the result that the modest six-parter quickly grew into something as big as, and even more ambitious than, *Life on Earth*. Instead of examining one specific area in each programme, suggested Attenborough, why not cover the whole planet, with one programme on deserts of the world, one on jungles, another on oceans, and so on? The project, given the seal of approval by Christopher Parsons (by then Head of the Natural History Unit), was offered to the Controller of BBC1 in May 1979, along with several other programmes.

'Planet Earth' (its new name) was listed under 'Long-term projects' as something which might be transmitted in four years' time or more as the legitimate son of *Life on Earth*. The proposal identified the three most important factors in the success of the earlier series:

(a)   David Attenborough;

Christopher Parsons The pioneer of many new wildlife productions (*P. Morris*)

David Attenborough A vital factor in the new series (*David Attenborough/BBC Enterprises*)

Wildlife spectacular Dramatic scenes such as this wildebeest migration were expected of *The Living Planet*, following the success of *Life on Earth* (AW)

(b) photographic excellence in covering a wide diversity of life forms – many never seen before;

(c) a broad story theme which unfolds over the series as a whole.

It went on: ' "Planet Earth" will have these three elements and yet need cover little of the subject material already seen in *Life on Earth*.' Also enclosed was a draft synopsis for the series put together by David Attenborough, which showed how far the concept had developed in the months since it had first been discussed. It was now based on the geological cycle of volcanic eruption, continental drift, erosion and deposition, and illustrated each stage by looking at the different physical conditions which have resulted from it, and the ways in which animals and plants have adapted to these conditions.

With such an outstanding pedigree, it was not a hard job to persuade the Controller of BBC1 that 'Planet Earth' should be granted a budget. The only question was whether the viewing public would see it as no more than an attempt to cash in on *Life on Earth* and find a use for all the thousands of feet of film which were left over from the earlier series. David Attenborough was certain that a view of nature from an entirely different angle was fully justified:

'Nothing succeeds like success, and when you've got something demonstrably working well you ought to capitalise on it. We felt that there was another way of looking at natural history than that shown in *Life on Earth*. That series had in fact been regarded at first by many people as being a very oddball way of surveying the subject; there were even those who thought it was old-fashioned, unscientific and positively Victorian to study the animal kingdom family by family, first molluscs, then insects, fish, reptiles, birds and so on. Even so it worked well enough, and so for the second series we employed the alternative method of dividing the world up into ecosystems.

'After *Life on Earth* I didn't relish the prospect of going back to making the occasional 30-minute programme here and there. I had got my teeth into this subject and I knew there was an entire aspect of the natural world which hadn't yet been dealt with on television. Originally I planned to concentrate more on the geological side of things, but Richard had his own ideas and in the end we combined the two approaches. I knocked together a three-page synopsis, keeping fairly vague about the exact areas we were going to cover – you should never commit yourself too far on your first synopsis! All the same, I suspected that we wouldn't have a great deal of trouble getting approval for the series. Persuading the network Controllers to take on *Life on Earth* had been difficult because it was a new and unknown concept. In the end, of course, it didn't cost the viewer a penny and made a profit for the BBC which was used to finance other programmes, so naturally enough they were eager to begin a new series which would put more money into production. By offering the same presenter and a good proportion of the same team, there was a more than even chance that we would be given the money.'

A Controller does not simply bestow his approval on a new project; he also grants it a certain budget to cover the costs of production, and this has to be accurately calculated before any approval is given. In the case of *The Living Planet* (the new title of the series) this was a straightforward matter, because the new budget could be closely modelled on the one for *Life on Earth*, with a slight increase to account for inflation. The sum arrived at was £1.5 million, to be paid in annual portions over three years. As an estimated budget it is remarkably modest, especially when one considers that it eventually filled 11 hours of prime television time and paid for itself handsomely. Compared with the reckless extravagances of the film industry it is a miniscule total. On top of this, however, were the unseen costs, such as BBC overheads, the use of BBC camera equipment, the salaries of members of BBC staff and the vast resources of

Volcano spectacular Living geology was an important new ingredient (*NK*)

Insect spectacular This camouflaged insect of Borneo is part of a world we seldom see (*AW*)

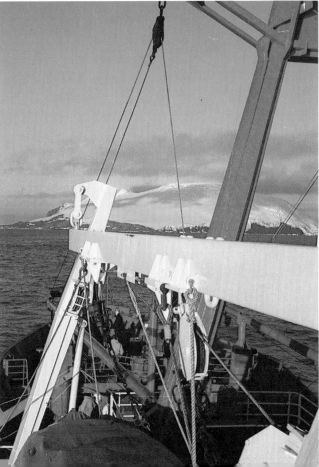

BBC studios and expertise. With all this taken into account, the cost rises past the £3 million mark.

The budget estimate, together with a greatly enlarged synopsis, was presented to the Controller of BBC1 in September 1979 at what is called an 'Offers' meeting. It came as no surprise when the Controller agreed to the proposals, which included not only the budget but the number of staff members involved and a time limit. It was thought that the first programme would be transmitted early in 1984, a forecast which proved entirely accurate. This allowed a year for David Attenborough to spend in writing the individual scripts (one each month) and just over three years for the production. Filming would officially begin on 1 January 1981 although, as it turned out, opportunities arose which had to be seized before then. In the late autumn of 1980, the Royal Navy offered berths for a film crew on board a ship which was sailing to the South Atlantic calling at the Falkland Islands, South Georgia and Antarctica itself. This was the sort of fortuitous invitation which might never come again, and it was quickly accepted, even though there was no definite plan for using the material that would result from it.

Falklands Christmas Thanks to the Royal Navy, a film crew reached the remote South Atlantic: (left, top) Government House, Port Stanley; (left, bottom) Elephant seals on South Georgia, the South Sandwich Islands seen from the deck of HMS Endurance, a naval helicopter landing after a hard day's filming (*NK/BBC Enterprises*)

Ian Calvert Assistant producer (*AW*)

Ned Kelly Experienced producer and intrepid mountaineer (*NK*)

The Making of The Living Planet

Before a script could be written, the final shape of the series had to be decided upon. David Attenborough's revised synopsis had listed 13 programmes, but these were condensed into 12. Some subjects – deserts, jungles, oceans, islands, temperate forests and grasslands – were clear-cut and could not be confused with anything else. Others overlapped each other and were harder to define precisely. Originally, Attenborough had proposed separate programmes on volcanoes, mountains and the lands of snow and ice, but these were now conflated into two. The opening film, an introduction to the building of the Earth, was bound to examine volcanoes and, as a direct result, mountains as well. Snow and ice were sufficiently varied topics to merit a programme of their own. Then there was fresh water: in the original draft, this film was intended to cover swamps, but Richard Brock felt strongly that an entire programme should be devoted to the margins of the land, which included estuaries, beaches, cliffs and mangrove swamps. This would mean omitting a subject dear to David Attenborough's heart – caves – but after much discussion he agreed that there was not enough material to fill a 55-minute programme. The last two were bold and original topics, one studying the life of the skies, and the other the impact of Man upon the natural world.

Hugh Miles Tough, determined and an expert at fieldcraft (*Stephen Bolwell/Agilis Pictures*)

As David Attenborough settled down at the beginning of 1980 to write his dozen scripts, Richard Brock stretched his wings as executive producer. First of all he had to assemble his team, recruiting both BBC staff and freelance operators who worked to short-term contracts. Eager to get hold of the best and most reliable professionals, he had already approached two men for whom he had great respect, Ned Kelly and Hugh Miles. Kelly was an experienced producer and an expert on mountaineering and icy conditions; far happier in the wastes of the Arctic than at a desk, he had once climbed Mount Everest with an international expedition. Hugh Miles, another rugged and independent character, had been a BBC cameraman for ten years before becoming a freelance film-maker, and had quickly gained an outstanding reputation. Both men were eager to be involved in the making of *The Living Planet*.

Three producers were needed for the series, each to be responsible for four programmes. 'You might be able to define the perfect person on paper', Richard Brock says, 'but in the end it depends on who is available. A producer for a wide-ranging series like this has got to be prepared to set aside three years of his life to the making of it, and have the right sort of qualifications. On the one hand he has to be tough and resourceful enough to lead trips into remote areas such as the Arctic Circle or the Sahara Desert, and on the other he has to have expert biological knowledge so that he can get the best filming out of each location. When you have someone like Ned Kelly on hand, you can rely on his huge experience of operating in inhospitable places. However, he is not a trained biologist, so he was assigned Ian Calvert (who is) as his assistant producer. The third producer, besides Ned and myself, was Andrew Neal, who has a strong academic background and some experience of overseas filming trips. My assistant producer was Adrian Warren, and Andrew worked with Richard Matthews.'

Andrew Neal One of whose first trips was to the Sahara Desert with **Martin Saunders** (*AW*)

Sharing out the 12 programmes was a matter of finding the right man for each job. Richard Brock himself was particularly interested in oceans and rivers, reckoning that, as executive producer, he would

Adrian Warren Pilot, balloonist, climber, aerial adventurer – and assistant producer (*AW*)

only have the time to make two programmes. His assistant Adrian Warren was an experienced enough film-maker to look after another two almost unaided. As Adrian's consuming passion was well-known to be for all things aerial, he took on the skies and the jungles, which gave him scope for some adventurous rope-work high on the rain-forest canopy. Ned Kelly was eminently well-suited to the programmes on mountains and volcanoes, the realms of snow and ice and the northern forests; having produced a BBC series on Charles Darwin, he also had the necessary experience to deal with oceanic islands. So when Andrew Neal arrived in Bristol in the Spring of 1980 he found that his four programmes had been decided for him. He was not in the least put out, for he had a wide knowledge of desert life, while his assistant Richard Matthews had been born and raised on the grasslands of Africa. The remaining two programmes, on coasts and cities, were relatively unexplored areas, and offered the chance of some original film-making.

The making of a series as ambitious as *The Living Planet* has to be meticulously planned. Once filming starts, activity becomes hectic, with producers and film crews flying to all corners of the Earth and often spending no more than a few days at a time in the office. It is vital that there should be a still point at the centre of all this bustle, someone who keeps a close eye on the schedules and the budget, and who can sort out day-to-day problems as they arise. That person is the unit manager, although the man involved, Andrew Buchanan, could scarcely have been described as still. He soon became celebrated for his habit of firing off a memo, following it up with a slightly altered version, and capping both with a telephone call. Together with the rest of the production team, Beth Huntley, Nicola Holford, Marney Shears and Diana Richards, he formed the core of the office staff, more often than not to be found in the Unit's headquarters in Bristol.

Vital support Unit manager Andrew Buchanan with 'the girls': from left to right, Nicola Holford, Andrew Buchanan, Diana Richards, Marney Shears, Beth Huntley (*AW*)

The filming itself fell into three categories. The first, and most labour-intensive, involved David Attenborough in front of the camera. In order to give a balance and a sense of continuity to the series, he must appear on the screen, speaking to the viewer, at fairly regular intervals throughout each programme. His khaki-clad figure, radiating a unique kind of personable enthusiasm, is a reassuring sign to the audience that they are in safe hands. To judge from the synopsis he would need to be shown standing in an extraordinary variety of locations, including the Himalayas, the Amazon jungle, Antarctica and the Sahara Desert. A full film crew would have to accompany him to record his pieces of commentary in synchronisation with the camera (known in the trade as 'sync' filming). The resulting party would therefore consist of a cameraman and his assistant, a sound recordist, a producer, and sometimes a production assistant – not to mention Attenborough himself.

Richard Brock was glad to be able to get hold of many of the BBC staff who had worked so successfully on *Life on Earth*. There are several cameramen and sound men based in Bristol, but none works exclusively for the Natural History Unit; they may be filming gorillas one week, football the next and current affairs the week after that. Their time has to be booked up many months in advance. For a series as big as *The Living Planet* two main cameramen were booked for the first year, but somehow stayed for three-and-a-half years. Cameramen Martin Saunders and Hugh Maynard and sound recordist Lyndon 'Dicky' Bird had all travelled extensively with Attenborough during the making of *Life on Earth*, and had proved themselves to be not only excellent technicians but also cheerful and resourceful companions when the going got tough. Saunders and Bird now formed the main crew, and Maynard, with recordist Keith Rodgerson, the second string.

Almost all sync pieces were filmed by one or other of these teams, but the cameramen were also used whenever possible to take sequences of the animals themselves. This specialist filming was the largest category of the shooting for the series, simply because it is mostly about creatures other than David Attenborough. In fact, Attenborough himself takes little active part in any of the location filming, except where he himself is talking to the camera. This is something he regrets, but the budget simply will not stretch to allow extra passengers on any trip. Species shooting is mainly done 'mute' (without sound recording, which is dubbed on after editing), and the crew is cut to the bare minimum, consisting of the cameraman, with or without an assistant, and sometimes a producer. When it is impossible to use one of the BBC staff, a freelance film-maker has to be hired. Richard Brock had worked with many freelancers over the

The key three (Far left) Dicky Bird, sound recordist, on location (with microphone): (right) cameramen Hugh Maynard and (bottom) Martin Saunders

years, and was familiar with their individual skills.

The third type of filming can loosely be called 'laboratory work'. When the script calls for a sequence on the leaf-cutter ant, or the inside of a termite mound, or the behaviour of a small fish on the river-bed, these will more than likely have to be filmed under artificial conditions. Companies such as Oxford Scientific Films and London Scientific Films, and freelancers such as Rodger Jackman and Stephen Bolwell, have developed extremely sophisticated techniques for shooting apparently impossible subjects using tanks and specially designed sets in their own studios. Reptiles, fish and insects can be flown thousands of miles from their native habitat and encouraged to go about their normal business in the seclusion of a laboratory. This sort of highly detailed work makes it possible for David Attenborough to illustrate many points about animals that simply cannot be made in the wild.

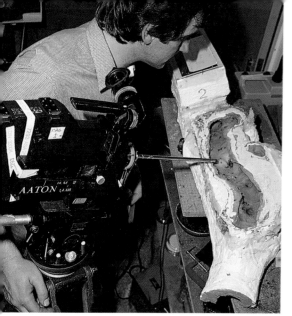

Ants and pants Hugh Maynard films leaf-cutting ants in the comfort of a Bristol studio (*Hugh Maynard/BBC Enterprises*); freelance cameraman Stephen Bolwell (below) found Brazil a lot steamier (*Hugh Maynard/Agilis Pictures*)

As Richard Brock assembled his team and David Attenborough pondered on his draft scripts, a third force was moving into action, looking for the means to sustain all this activity – money. A budget had already been approved by the Controller, but this did not mean that all the hard cash would come out of the BBC coffers. By providing the resources – staff, expertise and technical equipment – the BBC was providing perhaps a half of the required sum. The rest has to be raised by selling the series to foreign television companies and by attracting some well-heeled co-producers. The biggest market outside Britain was clearly the United States, where Warner Brothers had shared the production costs of *Life on Earth*. The BBC's own Co-Productions Department on this occasion made a deal with Time–Life Video, who invested money in the new series, providing another quarter of the budget.

The remainder was gathered by another of the Corporation's agents, BBC Enterprises. This body acts in many ways as an independent investor; *The Living Planet* was offered as a commercial proposition by the Head of the Natural History Unit, Christopher Parsons, and not surprisingly was snapped up. John Kelly of BBC Enterprises explains:

'We concentrate on selling BBC productions to the television networks in Europe. The hard work has to be done before production actually starts, which means that we haven't got anything concrete to show anybody except the original synopsis. In the case of *The Living Planet* we also had to convince our customers that the new series was going to be even better than *Life on Earth*. We gradually came to concentrate on the Norwegian and Swedish television corporations NRK and STV because we knew that natural history films are very popular in those countries. In addition to this, parts of the programme on the northern forests were going to be filmed in Scandinavia and Lapland, and the Norwegian producer Hans Christian Alsvik was going to help with the research and setting up of locations. After six months of negotiation, which included a trip to Bristol to meet Richard Brock and his team, the Norwegians and the Swedes signed a joint production agreement with us. This meant that they invested money in the project in return for the right to tailor the completed series when it is shown in their countries, in order to emphasise the parts that are of more local interest to them.'

After this major agreement, John Kelly also sold the series to five other European countries who would not be so strongly involved in production – Italy, Spain, Portugal, Germany and the Netherlands. Networks in other countries were willing to to pay a premium before the series was made so that they could be sure of securing the rights for screening it as soon as it became available. Although all of them were free to modify the series slightly for their own consumption, there was no question of them interfering with the conception or the production of it: responsibility for this remained firmly in Bristol. So the budget began to fall into place like a jigsaw, allowing *The Living Planet* to pay its own way before a single programme had been completed.

WRITING AND RESEARCH

How a programme takes shape

The book of *Life on Earth* sold spectacularly well throughout the world, earning for David Attenborough a massive sum in royalties. He spent a large part of this, prosaically enough, on his family home in Richmond. He and his wife had lived there comfortably for 30 years and decided that it needed a few repairs. The repairs grew into a major job of reconstruction: the roof had to be taken off, and then it was discovered that the house had no foundations.

Oblivious of the rubble, scaffolding and concrete mixers, he sat down in his study to write the first draft for *The Living Planet* (still known at that stage as 'Planet Earth'). He had given himself a year in which to write the whole series, which meant completing one programme every month. For background information and inspiration, he has a huge library of books and papers to draw on; for technique he has his long years of experience of writing for television and radio. Yet to outsiders it can seem a mysterious, almost alchemical, process:

'Before I start I have to get the subjects of each programme clear in my mind, and resolve any problems of overlapping. Does the tundra, for example, belong in the programme on snow and ice or in the one on the northern forests? Then I settle down and think about the first script for a couple of weeks, reading all round each topic. I've been travelling all over the world on and off for 30 years now, so I've got a memory filled with ideas for how I might treat each type of ecosystem, and some fairly firm opinions as well. The first thing is to decide what are the fundamental characteristics of the plants and animals that live in one particular environment. What are the problems they have to deal with? With a subject like deserts, that's easy to answer, because the problems are that it's too hot and there's not enough water so that their lives are taken up with coping with heat and drought. It's more difficult when you come to the jungles and try to define the problems of living there. I decided that the major problem was simply diversity; there are so many forms of life in a tropical rainforest that plants and animals are engaged in fierce competition with each other.

'People don't carry away many ideas from a television programme, so the number of points you can put over are limited. It is a mistake to try and cram in too many ideas. You have to make it perfectly clear as to what the one or two important issues are, and then you have to illustrate them in as many dramatic ways as you can. If there is a strong narrative thread too, then that is an absolute godsend, because you don't just want a facile or illogical succession of images. I can't pretend, for example, that I'm particularly knowledgeable about the sky. But the producer was Adrian Warren, and he is: he's a mad keen pilot, parachutist, mountaineer and so on, and he had a lot of exciting suggestions to make. In the end I got as much, if not more, pleasure out of writing the script for "The Sky Above" as I did from any of the others, because it came out as a nice idea for a televsion programme. I hit upon the scheme of starting only one inch above the ground, seeing how creatures get into the air, and gradually getting higher until it ended up in the stratosphere. That was a strong story-line, and there were all kinds of spectacular ways in which we could illustrate it.

'After the two weeks of thinking and planning, I spend the next two weeks writing the script itself. All the time I try to imagine what I would be seeing on the television screen: what would be the succession of images that appears? The first draft is usually about 30 pages long and is not merely a sketch. It has to be written in very considerable detail, because I know that it is not going to be filmed in sequence and therefore everything has to be right, even down to the tenses of the statements I am going to make in front of the camera. Nouns are another snare for the scriptwriter. If I'm filming on location I may want to say, for example, "This is a Gila monster which behaves in such-and-such a manner." But when I work out the script I will realise that the Gila monster will already have appeared in a mute shot and will have been introduced by name. Therefore for my sync shot I must use not the proper noun but the pronoun: "*It* behaves in such-and-such a manner." That's just the kind of detail

A Gila monster To be handled with care (*Diana Richards/BBC Enterprises*)

The words Subject to alteration, but always as precise as possible (*Diana Richards*)

which can snarl you up if you're not careful at this stage.

'Of course, the script doesn't stay in this pristine condition because the next step is to give it to a producer. He reads through it, makes suggestions, turns it round a bit and finds some better examples of particular pieces of behaviour. He may give it to a bright chap such as Ian Calvert who can burrow into the subject in research laboratories and libraries to a degree that I can't possibly match in the two weeks that I've got for my thinking. Ian and others came up with several tricks that I had missed. I didn't know, for example, about the red-cockaded woodpecker of the southern USA and its ploy of keeping intruders from its nest by covering the surrounding bark with resin. That fitted very well into the programme on northern forests.

'So the script gets altered first in order to include this new material. I alter it even more when we get out on location and find that things aren't quite as I had imagined. And I alter it finally when I come to write the commentary. The important point is that at no time are we without a script; we have always got a plan to work to, and if we don't *need* to change it, then we don't. But if there is no plan to start off with, we are sunk. I'm also very particular about transcripts, and as soon as I've filmed a piece on location, one of the producer's assistants will type out exactly what I have said, give me a carbon copy and I will stick that in my master file. I carry all the scripts with me on every trip in a great thick file, because all of them are being modified continually. I do this because at any time we might have the opportunity to film something that was unplanned, and we will need to know exactly what are the lead-in and the lead-out so that the new piece can be dovetailed in. After every day's filming I sit down and make sure that my master file is up-to-date.'

The script for the first programme, 'The building of the Earth', arrived on Ned Kelly's desk at the end of August 1980. On the front page was this note:

'This script is only a skeleton, to show the structure of the programme. The nature of the flesh – the details within each section – has been left deliberately vague, for it will only become apparent when research is completed on each segment and filming is started. Consequently it is extremely unlikely that any single sentence in this written narration will survive in the final film, since it must be modified in the light of the sequences that we finally obtain. The text here serves only to show the sequence of ideas.'

'The sequence of ideas' is a modest phrase, but in it lies the clue to David Attenborough's enduring success as a popular communicator. He would be the first to admit that there are gaps in his knowledge of biology or ecology, and that he is not always able to keep up with the current thinking on every topic he suggests (the range of specialised learning today is so huge that he would be scarcely human if he could). His most important single contribution to any programme or series is the mapping out of that 'sequence of ideas' which will probably remain as the basic plot when it appears on the screen months or years later. To do this, he takes vast and complex subjects and boils them down in his unique way into something very simple.

The structure he devised for Programme One is an excellent example of this. Being the first, it has to show what the series will be like; it also has to discuss enormous topics such as mountain-building, volcanic activity, animal and plant adaptation to altitude, and the forces of erosion. David Attenborough set the first scene on a ridge 16 000 feet high in the Himalayas – the roof of the world. The narrator comes into view, trudging up the slope (exaggerating his breathlessness in order to emphasise the lack of oxygen), and introduces the viewer to this harsh terrain with its thin air and low temperatures. Then he turns and picks up a fragment of rock containing an ammonite. This, he tells us, is the fossilised shell of an ancient creature which once lived in the sea: how could it have got to the heart of Asia, hundreds of miles away from the sea and several miles above its level?

The performance Filmed in the Himalayas – with heavy breathing added! *(NK)*

This question moves him neatly on to the subject of how the mountains were formed by the folding and lifting of a sea-bed millions of years ago, and how the forces of nature have altered, and are still altering, the face of the Earth. After this, he considers how the landscape produced by all this mighty activity becomes colonised by plants and animals. First algae grows, and insects come to feed on it; then spiders prey upon the insects, and a food chain is established. The programme ends as it began in mountainous scenery near the

snowline, with the narrator giving a lead into the second part of the series, which concentrates on 'The frozen world' of snow and ice.

As a sequence of ideas, this was striking and uncomplicated. But David Attenborough saw one major weakness. 'It is very important', he wrote, 'that geology should not overshadow biology. That would give a false impression of the series as a whole, which will, of course, be primarily concerned with plants and animals in different environments. I judge that the balance between the two ingredients in this programme at any rate should be about half and half.' In other words, if the series was to capitalise on the proven success of *Life on Earth*, it had got to show, in the first ten minutes, that it was about natural history and not about geology. But how could this be done when the main part of the programme's story was about fossils and volcanoes?

Kelly and Attenborough pondered the problem. Obviously they had to start in the Himalayas, in order to keep the basic outline of the script. So they decided to begin the programme at the bottom of the Kali Gandaki Gorge, the deepest valley in the world. Although the valley floor is about 7000 feet above sea level, its sides rise up to 26 000 feet and the peaks of two gigantic mountains, Dhaulagiri and Annapurna. As before, the narrator appears puffing his way towards the camera, but now he is beside the narrow river that has cut its way right through the mountains.

The next few minutes are devoted to a simulation of a slow climb out of the gorge, observing on the way the rich variety of wildlife to be found on its slopes. At different altitudes rhododendrons, red pandas, blood pheasants, langur monkeys, griffon vultures, martens and bears are all adapted to and dependent upon their particular environment. As the narrator travels ever higher, the air gets thinner and colder, and he can draw our attention to the greater difficulties of sustaining life. Only thick-furred animals such as the yak and the elusive snow leopard can thrive here – along with the hardy Sherpa villagers. At length we reach the top of the gorge, where the narrator picks up the ammonite and the geology lesson can begin.

This opening sequence lasts for 12 minutes in the completed programme, and it is vital in establishing several things about the series as a whole. The ecological thread running through *The Living Planet* has been emphasised, and the viewer has been hooked by some stunning pictures of animals. The glimpse of the Sherpa village has suggested that man himself is going to be examined in forthcoming programmes as well as wildlife – a point which sets the new series clearly apart from *Life on Earth*. Lastly, the viewer has seen that David Attenborough is there on film moving through these different habitats, and is going to be the guiding spirit of the series.

The Kali Gandaki Gorge The deepest valley in the world (*NK*)

Martin Saunders in the Himalayas (*NK*)

A Sherpa village Man had an important role in the new series (*NK*)

The ironing out of this sequence was the first stage in Ned Kelly's shaping work. Afterwards, he was able with Richard Brock to look at the way the story-line developed and see how the research work already done could be fitted into it. Research had been started even before the script had arrived, and attractive possibilities were investigated while the opportunity was there. For example, researcher John Waters had ferreted out some details of a parrot which bathed in the smoke of a volcano in Nicaragua. This was an interesting instance of special adaptation to an environment, for it would seem that the bird had learnt that the sulphurous fumes from the volcano killed off the parasites in its feathers. However, the idea was reluctantly dropped, partly because there was no natural place for it in the programme, and partly because of the volatile political situation in Nicaragua. Cameramen are accustomed to the dangers of sharks and polar bears, but civil wars are a different matter.

The next priority was some spectacular footage of film featuring, if possible, David Attenborough beside an active volcano. But this was late 1980, and all of the world's great volcanoes seemed to be slumbering peacefully. Ned Kelly was forced to bide his time, chafing at the hold-up:

'You don't want to delay for too long for fear that it might not happen at all, because then you're really stuck and have to start pushing things right to the end of your filming schedule. So we were constantly monitoring what volcano activity there was. One of our contacts worked for a travel agency, and ran what he called an "Icelandic hot-line". He had friends sitting in the seismological stations in Iceland who had promised to ring him up if anything exciting happened. Eventually one November morning he phoned me to say that the volcano at Krafla – a huge fire fountain – had started erupting and looked set for a big display.'

Kelly and his assistant Marney Shears had all their plans laid, and swiftly went into action. An Icelandic film crew was alerted, for it was much too short notice to book a BBC team, and a light aeroplane was hired, to be ready and waiting for them in Reykjavik. David Attenborough hurriedly packed his bags and he and Kelly left Heathrow Airport at six o'clock that evening. They reached Reykjavik at midnight, transferred to the light plane and flew on through the night in the teeth of a howling blizzard. Soon they were able to see the great red glow of the volcano in the distance, even though they were still 80 miles away. On landing at Akureyri they were met by the film crew who had hired a Land Rover, into which they bundled to continue their seemingly endless journey. When they had left London, the temperature was 60°F: here it was 0°F.

After five hours in the Land Rover, they arrived in a small village near Krafla at 6 a.m. It was still pitch dark so there was time for

The Krafla Fire Fountain sends up a jet of molten lava

breakfast and a cup of coffee, after which they set off on the final stage, this time aboard snowmobiles. At long last they reached the Fire Fountain itself. Great wafts of sulphurous smoke filled the air and tiny fragments of red-hot ash rained down as they began filming. Kelly and Attenborough had by this time had no sleep for nearly 30 hours, but they kept hard at it throughout the day, capturing the different aspects of the spectacular scene before them: this was their chance, and they had to make the most of it. That evening, as they slid across the snow on the way to their hotel, they met two snowmobiles going in the opposite direction. An American voice called out 'Hey! Is that David Attenborough? We've just flown in from New York to film this Fire Fountain too!' The man on the Icelandic hot-line clearly had customers on both sides of the Atlantic.

Despite the fumes, hot ash, icy cold and gales, David Attenborough records his piece in front of the camera (*NK/BBC Enterprises*)

With this mad scramble completed, Ned Kelly knew that at least he had David Attenborough *and* a volcano safely in the can, but he was still anxious to show many other kinds of volcanic activity in the programme. There were no other dramatic eruptions and, besides, the *Living Planet* team did not have the time or the money to film it all themselves. Was there any stock footage in the Natural History Unit library which could be used? Rosi Crane, the Unit's film librarian, had been called in on the series early so that the producers could draw on her encyclopedic knowledge of the library's contents and search for film worldwide. If a sequence was already available, if it was dramatic enough and – best of all – it it hadn't been shown on television before, then a lot of travelling expense could be saved. Rosi Crane could, alas, find little on volcanoes that was new. Then she called to mind a letter that Richard Brock had passed on to her several months earlier. It had come from a Frenchman called Maurice Krafft, who had originally been offering material for a *Life on Earth* programme back in 1978. Krafft was a specialist in the filming of volcanoes, so she immediately wrote to him with a lengthy 'shopping list' of what was needed. He replied that he had such a vast amount of film to choose from that they had better come over to France and see it for themselves.

When Rosi Crane arrived at his house near the Swiss border she was amazed to find what amounted to a volcano museum. The lives of Maurice Krafft and his wife were completely devoted to the filming and examination of volcanic activity wherever it occurred in the world, and the collecting of lava samples and other memorabilia. As many tribes who live near volcanoes tend to place a bad luck curse on anyone taking pieces of lava as souvenirs, they were running a certain risk. Another much more gruesome trophy was the pair of manacles worn by a criminal who was the only survivor of the catastrophic volcanic explosion on the Island of Martinique in 1902.

Equally astonishing, however, was the range of film available. There were volcanoes exploding, underground lava flows and eruptions galore – many of which had since become inactive – and altogether it was what Ned Kelly called 'a real pot of gold'. Furthermore, the Kraffts were obviously skilled and professional film-makers who knew how to build up a sequence properly, how to vary the angles, how to film cutaway shots and how to edit neatly. None of their extraordinary work had ever been seen on British television before, and so another big problem seemed to have been solved in one fell swoop.

Brine flies Part of the strange community of insects living in the hot springs of Yellowstone National Park

No programme about volcanoes would be complete without at least glimpses of the two most famous sites of all – Krakatoa (the cause, in 1883, of the biggest explosion in recorded history) and Mount St Helens, in the state of Washington in the USA. The latter was easy enough to get to, but filming on Krakatoa, the remains of which lie in the Sunda Strait west of Java, would mean a long and expensive trip to Indonesia, almost on the other side of the world. What other work could be done on the way there which might make it a more economic proposition? Nothing stood out, and the trip was shelved for a year so that the various possibilities could be sorted out with the other producers.

Mount St Helens The volcanic mountain which blew up in 1980 *(NK)*

Meanwhile, Ned Kelly was considering what kinds of animals could be brought into the action. This was still an important gap, because all the geological information had to be punctuated with some animal activity. David Attenborough's script featured the hot springs in Yellowstone Park in the USA, where water percolating down to the molten lava is superheated and shot to the surface again. Although the water is still nearly at boiling point when it emerges, a whole community of tiny insects – flies, mites and spiders – lives and breeds here. Ned Kelly knew where to find the perfect contact for this sort of work, a man with whom he had once done some film-

The biggest bang of all The crew on Krakatoa, the scene of a gigantic volcanic explosion in 1883 (*NK*)

ing and whose research centred on these hot springs. He had diverted part of a spring channel on to a raised platform so that a camera could comfortably be placed at surface level. This was an ideal place for filming, easy to get to and with everything set up for cameraman David Thompson of Oxford Scientific Films.

By 1982 the trip to Indonesia was taking shape, and changing rapidly into a round-the-world expedition that would last for a month and a half. First of all assistant producer Ian Calvert set off westwards via the United States and Hawaii, finding suitable locations, contacting experts and arranging for filming permission. When virtually everything was settled, Ned Kelly, David Attenborough and the film crew flew eastwards until they met Calvert in Indonesia. This complex journey (described in more detail in a later chapter) produced a huge harvest of good film, which provided material for at least three of the final programmes. After Krakatoa they made the voyage to Komodo, a tiny island in a long chain east of Java where fierce storms and tidal rips are everyday hazards. Here they filmed the giant dragon lizards, which David Attenborough had first encountered during his *Zoo Quest* expeditions 25 years earlier, and which were an important example of isolated adaptation to be used in the programmes on oceanic islands. In Queensland, Australia, and New Zealand they shot sequences for Andrew Neal's programme on coastlines.

The fearsome dragon lizards of Komodo thrive on a diet of meat – fortunately they didn't develop a taste for film-makers! (*NK*)

After a highly convoluted series of manoeuvres, the party reached one of the remote Gilbert Islands in mid-Pacific, where they were greeted by the choir of the local village, who waded out to the boat and carried them shoulder-high to the shore draped with garlands. Finally, they arrived in Hawaii, the last leg of their marathon. Here, paradoxically, they were back in the realm of volcanoes, filming in the deep underground tunnels formed by lava flows which had cooled on top and crusted over. Ian Calvert had been in contact with a scientist who had spent several years studying the communities of weird insects that live in these caverns, and he led the crew into the recesses of this completely lightless world. After centuries of darkness the insects have lost both their sight and their ability to fly. The intrusion of a camera crew, together with a set of powerful lights and heavy generators, must have been a rare shock for them.

Just as Ned Kelly was able to film material for his fellow-producers during this trip, so they were able to help in the shaping of his own programmes. This often arrived unexpectedly. Richard Brock, for instance, was in the midst of his research on oceans when he came across a film of the primitive animal life which has developed in the deepwater trenches off the Galapagos Islands in the Pacific. Volcanic vents in the trenches release steady streams of heat, and this has attracted a whole group of unique creatures – species of giant clam and deep sea worm – which subsisted on the chemical products of underground rather than solar energy. These animals had only just been discovered by scientists, and had rarely been filmed before. Here was a perfect example of adaptation to a volcanic habitat which had not figured in David Attenborough's original script, and Ned Kelly jumped at the chance of including it in 'The building of the Earth'.

Thus Programme One began to take visible form. As shooting and research continued, writer and producer discussed the script, altering it where necessary, fitting in new ideas and checking the accuracy of every fact. By the Christmas of 1982, things were far enough advanced for a rough-cut version of the final programme, called an 'assembly', to be screened before an audience of *Living Planet* staff, members of the Natural History Unit, and promotions men from BBC Enterprises. This gave a chance for everybody to judge how the series was progressing, and make their comments known to the producers.

But it would be misleading to suggest that Programme One jogged happily along from A towards Z in a logical order. It is almost always impossible to shoot a film in its eventual chronological sequence: a run-down of Ned Kelly's timetable for 'The building of the Earth' shows what a jigsaw puzzle the schedule can turn into:

The crew arrive by sailing canoe at the island of Kiribati during their round-the-world trip (*NK*)

August 1980	First script arrives from David Attenborough
November 1980	Middle section, of a volcanic eruption, shot in Iceland
January 1982	Revised script completed
April 1982	Opening and closing sequences filmed in Nepal
October 1982	Middle sections filmed during world trip on Krakatoa and Hawaii
December 1982	Rough-cut 'assembly' screened in Bristol
January 1984	Final version transmitted on BBC1

Obviously filming opportunities have to be grabbed whenever they appear: volcanoes cannot spout lava to order, rhododendrons only bloom once a year, and monsoons are to be avoided if possible. The further you travel from the Equator, the shorter are the warm seasons, so if there is filming to be done in the High Arctic, the producer has to bear in mind that the summers there last for only six weeks. Nevertheless, as David Attenborough knows full well, it can be thoroughly disconcerting to be speaking to the camera on a Himalayan mountainside without any concrete idea of what will precede or follow that particular piece of commentary. Every programme also has to be linked with the next in the series – another matter for the producers to keep in close consultation about.

With most of the major location work completed to his satisfaction, Ned Kelly now found himself having to spend an increasing amount of his time in the *Living Planet* headquarters in Bristol. Whereas 1982 had been a year of hectic travelling, 1983 was devoted to the final shaping and polishing of Programme One: it was, after all, to be the flagship of the series and deserved special attention. The assembly which had been shown at Christmas had been nearly complete as far as the editing of the film was concerned, but had little or no sound track except where David Attenborough had been shot on location 'in sync'. The laying down and mixing of eight different tracks and the adding of music and commentary are highly intricate – not to say laborious – jobs, and the producer has to keep a close eye on every stage of it. There was an additional headache in the case of 'The building of the Earth'. Because it dealt with vast and often unfilmable topics such as the movement of the tectonic plates of the Earth's crust or the causes of volcanic explosions, these had to be depicted in animated sequences of sufficiently high quality as not to jar with the rest of the film. The preparation of these was the work of graphic designer Margaret Perry, but she needed a great deal of technical information and advice to ensure that each sequence was correct.

Graphic designer Margaret Perry (*AW*)

On top of all this, of course, was the small matter of three other programmes to produce. David Attenborough had undertaken to complete one draft script every month, and hot on the heels of 'The building of the Earth' came Programme Two, 'The frozen world' (about snow and ice), Programme Three, 'The northern forests' and Programme Ten, 'Worlds apart' (about oceanic islands). The first of these was clearly going to be the most difficult to film, as it involved trips to both polar regions with their short summers, and work on it had to be started as soon as possible. As the transmission date approached, activity became more frenetic as the last pieces of each jigsaw were fitted into place.

That, in brief, is how one programme came to be made in the way that the British public first saw it in January 1984, nearly three-and-a-half years after its conception. It is the product of a great deal of research, which embroiders and improves on the original David Attenborough script without altering the fundamental plot. The producers are under no illusions about the value of Attenborough's ground-plan. 'When I get a script', says Andrew Neal, 'I read it through and may well feel that I could have done it myself, it seems so simple: I may even spot a scientific error. But that misses the point, which is to appreciate how he turns a big subject into a simple theme that any Joe Soap could follow when he watched it on the screen.'

The producer then goes through the script step-by-step, looking at the examples in fine detail. To find out current thinking and research, he taps the experts in each individual field from archaeology to zoology. With a three-year time scale there is the opportunity to get in touch with anyone in any part of the world who he may think can help. He can write to a university professor in New Zealand, for example, and it will only cost him the price of a stamp. While he is waiting for a reply he can be writing to 40 other professors in 40 other universities. In this way, a network of contacts and advisers is built up, and new ideas come to the surface.

At the same time, a number of freelance researchers is put on the trail of various possibilities. If a producer is lucky enough to find a willing helper who is actually on the spot, he can save himself a lot of travelling and be sure of getting a realistic answer to his queries. Cathy Mackenzie, a zoology graduate from Canada studying in Manaus, Brazil, was asked to find out about certain species of fish which Richard Brock wanted to include in his programme on rivers. John Waters, who was planning a backpacking holiday in South America, was given a long 'shopping list' of matters to investigate, including the real source of the River Amazon:

'David Attenborough's script for "Sweet fresh water" opened with

Kalahari bushmen They were uniquely adapted for life in the desert, but how would a camera crew survive? (*Diana Richards*)

him standing at the source of the Amazon. The scene needed to make a telling contrast between the fact that this was only a little bubbling spring and the fact that it was the start of the greatest river in the world. Richard Brock phoned me up and asked me, as I was going in that general direction anyway, if I would find a suitable (and authentic) location for filming this sequence. There are several places which claim to be the source of the Amazon, but I decided to visit the one given by the National Geographic Atlas, which was up in the Andes near a town called Araquipo. I arrived in the town and found an Englishman who lives there and takes tours into the mountains, one of which was billed as going to the source of the Amazon. We had a stupendous drive up the dirt roads into the High Andes, through some spectacular scenery to about 15 000 feet. But when we got there, it could have been anywhere. It looked more like a little stream in the Lake District than the beginning of a great river. A big disappointment.'

Whenever possible, producers like to do their own reconnaissance work, because only they know the precise questions they want to ask and the sort of locations they are looking for. Andrew Neal, for example, had done a great deal of travelling before a foot of film had been shot for his programmes. In February 1981 he flew to the USA to finalise arrangements for the filming of 'The baking deserts'. In less than four weeks he visited zoos and universities in Houston, San Antonio, Albuquerque, Phoenix, Tucson, Salt Lake City, San

Francisco, Los Angeles, San Diego and Washington DC. A month later he was in South Africa and Botswana finding out whether it would be possible to film the Bushmen of the Kalahari and, if so, how a BBC crew could travel into the desert. In May he was garnering further information for his first programme in Cairo, Tel Aviv and Jerusalem.

Meanwhile his assistant producer, Richard Matthews, was getting to grips with the programme for which he was going to be responsible, 'Seas of grass'. The draft script that he was given was the thinnest of the 12, grasslands and savannas being subjects about which David Attenborough is less wholeheartedly enthusiastic than he is about, say, the jungle. But Richard Matthews was born and bred in Africa, and knew many people in Kenya who would be useful in his research. He also flew to the Sudan, the United States (twice) and West Germany in his pursuit of information. In this way he built up a fat and very useful file on all the species that might be used as examples in the programme. Each animal has a section in which is recorded the latest research knowledge of its habitat, breeding pattern, physical characteristics, distribution and behaviour, culled from eminent specialists throughout the world. It is so tightly packed with up-to-date information that it has become an incomparable mine of source material for any number of future programmes on grasslands.

Once a location has been decided upon, formal permission has to be sought before filming can go ahead. In the early days of wildlife filming, African and South American countries welcomed camera crews with open arms, and gave them access to the most remote and beautiful parts of their landscapes with scarcely a raised eyebrow. But in recent years, the volume of film-making has grown enormously, and the crews can become something of a nuisance if they are continually invading National Parks in pursuit of ever more dramatic footage. Many governments have also seen that there is a lot of money to be made out of wildlife filming, and have understandably decided that some of that money should come their way. The result is that fees are often demanded from visiting film crews, and much tighter control is exercised over the granting of permits and visas.

This often leads to protracted and complicated negotiations with several different government departments at once, which a difference in language can make almost impossible to carry on. When Andrew Neal was planning a trip to the French-speaking part of the Sahara Desert in Niger, he was able to use Andrew Buchanan as organiser because of his fluent French. Buchanan relished the chance to get out of the office for a change, though he recognised that he had a formidable task. The subject of the filming was to be the camel caravans of the Sahara, but no one knew if there were any that were still regularly

The age of the train Camel trains still cross the Sahara Desert, as they have for centuries (*Hugh Maynard*)

crossing the desert in Niger. No one even knew how one went about getting filming permission in that far-flung country.

Andrew Buchanan set out on his 'recce' in October 1981, stopping first in Paris, to meet a French anthropologist, and then in Niamey, capital of Niger and terminus of the trans-Saharan motor route. He established where the caravans might be and who to go to for the necessary permits, and reported back to Andrew Neal. Throughout the next year telex messages and letters volleyed back and forth between the BBC and the Niger government departments. Stamped and signed letters of agreement were collected from the Ministry of Youth, Sports and Culture, and the Ministry of Foreign Affairs. A letter explaining the scope and aim of the entire series was sent from the Controller of BBC1 to the President of Niger's Military Council. A full curriculum vitae was drawn up for every member of the filming party. Finally, Andrew Buchanan flew to Niamey a week before the rest of the crew to obtain the actual permits for filming from the Ministry of the Interior.

Such a lengthy procedure is not at all unusual, and at least in this case the arrangements met relatively few obstacles. But in some countries the government officials seem to go out of their way to make the bureaucratic system as mystifying and time-wasting as possible. Ian Calvert has a particularly infuriating taste of this when trying to arrange filming in a country that shall remain nameless:

'They had developed an extraordinary system whereby you wrote to the man in charge of issuing permits and told him you were coming to get one. The issuing office is about 60 miles away from the capital city, so I flogged all the way over there and explained why I wanted the document. They replied that they would be happy to let me have a permit, but that I had to get it signed by the Head of their National Conservation body. This man, of course, was back in the capital. I told them that I had a taxi waiting, so that I could take the permit straight back to the capital, get it signed and carry on from there. Then he let me in on another little secret: once the document has been signed, it has to be stamped, and the only place that it can be stamped is, surprise, surprise, back here. In the end I shuttled between the two places about five times before I got what I wanted.'

Sometimes the difficulties placed in their way were so great that the producers had no choice but to throw up their hands and look elsewhere. The officials of the Soviet Union, as so often, proved singularly unhelpful. The Natural History Unit, in fact, has never succeeded in coming to a suitable agreement with the USSR over wildlife filming, and the new series did not manage to make a breakthrough. Richard Brock was keen to film at a Russian lake, one of the few places in the world where freshwater seals are to be found, and asked his secretary Beth Huntley to arrange it. She got nowhere: 'I worked almost exclusively for three months trying to get permission to film at the lake but it was impossible. They insisted that it was too near the Mongolian border and that there were military installations in the neighbourhood, and refused point blank. We even sent Andrew Buchanan over to Moscow to chat them up but it was to no avail.'

'Military installations' is the excuse given in most cases to people wanting to film in the Soviet Union. Richard Matthews encountered a slightly more subtle put-down:

'Initially they said that they welcomed the idea of our coming, and were great fans of David Attenborough. But what it all boils down to is: what can they get from us in return? For instance, for the 15 minute sequence that I was after, they wanted to be granted rights in the whole series. Then, to cap it all, they insisted on using Soviet cameramen who, judging from the film I've seen, don't seem to have invented the tripod yet and use very low quality film stock.'

Richard Brock was particularly disappointed that such a global series could not have included more material from the Soviet Union and China, but, as he put it: 'Nobody can say that we haven't tried!' In the end several sequences from library sources were used to show something of the wildlife of these two vast countries.

NUGGETS AND OTHERS
The cost of filming wildlife

'If you tread too carefully you will end up with a very ordinary programme. If you gamble too much you will spend all your money and end up with no programme at all.' Andrew Neal's warning words sum up the producer's dilemma. Each of the *Living Planet* producers was allocated one third of the total budget, with which he had to make four 55-minute films. There was enough there to enable him to take a certain number of risks, but not enough to be thoughtlessly extravagant. A few risks obviously had to be taken if anything original, unusual and spectacular was going to be included, but they can use up a lot of time and money without any guarantee of success. Somehow, the producer has to achieve a balance between the risky and the safe, between the unfamiliar and the conventional, between the expensive and the cheap.

The cheapest and simplest way of compiling a programme would have been to buy footage from private film-makers and libraries, or ransack the Natural History Unit's own library in Bristol. This contains a fantastic wealth of material which is continually being added to: the spare film from the making of *Life on Earth* alone took a whole year to catalogue. But using film that somebody else has shot is hardly the way to produce a series as ambitious and startling as *The Living Planet* was intended to be. The programmes will tend to become shaped by the material available, rather than the other way round. Inevitably a small amount of library film was used in the final product (about ten per cent), but only when it was considered absolutely necessary. For instance Maurice Krafft's stock of volcano film was unique and unmatchable, as was some of the footage of the rare snow leopard seen in 'The frozen world.'

The rest was original, shot either by BBC staff cameramen or by freelance film-makers specifically hired for the purpose. This is where the money began to be rapidly eaten away. People had to be paid, airline tickets had to be bought, transport had to be hired and hotel rooms had to be booked. If the location was no more exotic than, say, the Bingley Hall Exhibition Centre in Birmingham (where a cat show was filmed for the programme on cities), then the costs were minimal. But if a full crew of six or seven was flying to the depths of the Amazon jungle, it was an expensive undertaking.

So how much can a producer afford? The process of costing out an individual programme is bound to be a haphazard and instinctive one. No matter how carefully a shooting schedule is planned, it will inevitably be altered as research throws up new and more exciting ideas, and the original script is changed to accommodate them. The producer has no choice but to rely on a rule-of-thumb equation: he could allow £2000 for every minute of film that went into the completed programme. That was the rough sum worked out at the beginning of the series to cover travelling expenses and fees but not staff salaries. If he could be sure that a filming expedition was going to yield him five minutes of film, then he knew that the trip was worth £10 000.

Filming this cat show in Birmingham was quick and cheap; the Amazon jungle was a different matter (*RM/BBC Enterprises*)

Vast herds of wildebeest
migrate across Serengeti on
predictable routes every year,
and present a fairly simple
target for the film-maker (*AW*)

The figure was of course only an average – many projects were much cheaper and some were much more expensive. The producer could only set out with a relatively vague idea of the overall cost of his four programmes, and juggle his budget around to suit the changing circumstances. For example, Ned Kelly could foresee that three of his programmes – on volcanoes, oceanic islands, and snow and ice – were certain to involve journeys to some very remote places, such as the Arctic and Antarctic, and mid-Pacific islands. The fourth, however, was about the northern forest, most of which would be relatively easy to reach. By saving money on that, he might have a little extra to spend on the other three.

The 'little extra' is often used to finance those gambles which can, if successful, add stunning highlights to a series. 'When you set out to plan each programme', says Andrew Neal, 'you must try and discover if there is anything you can do that has never been done before. Is there a piece of behaviour, or a habitat, or even a species, that has never been filmed before? Of course, if something has never been done, the chances are that it will be something difficult, and if it's difficult, the chances are that it will be expensive. But unless you try you are not going to get the odd scoop, which is what the series depends on to a large extent. If we, with our comparatively large budget, can't film these things, who can?'

If these long shots succeed, they tend to be referred to triumphantly by producers as 'nuggets' – lumps of solid gold at the heart of their programmes. One such is the remarkable sequence in 'Seas of grass' which shows the migration of the white-eared kob across the Southern Sudan, in the course of which it is ambushed by the Murle tribesmen and killed in large numbers. A much easier task was to film the herds of wildebeest which migrate slightly further south, but this had already been done on several occasions with great skill by other camera crews. The unique difficulty posed by the kob migration was that it took place in an extremely remote part of Africa, and at a time of year when the heavy rains turned the black cotton soil into an impassable glue. But Richard Brock and Richard Matthews, the director of the programme, believed that it was a piece of film that justified a lot of time and money:

'A few people have tried to film this massive migration before, but either they have gone to the wrong place, or the kob have changed their route. The point about it was that it showed Man in harmony with nature. For years the Murle have depended on the herds of kob for food. The migration route of the kob takes them between two rivers. The rivers gradually flow closer together until they join, and if the rains have kept the rivers too high for the kob to cross elsewhere

Death in mid-stream (previous page) Murle tribesmen plunge into the water in pursuit of the migrating white-eared kob: (above) a few of the 5000 killed every year (*RM/BBC Enterprises*)

they have no choice but to swim across here. The junction is near a place called Pibor Post, and the Murle wait with their spears, killing about 100 to 300 kob on a good day. They kill about 5000 kob every year, sometimes scattered all up and down the rivers. That may seem a lot, but as there are about one million animals in the migration it doesn't make much of a dent in their numbers. However, without the kob the Murle would have a hard time surviving there. What they kill is dried and lasts them for several months, making the kob a vital part of their ecology.

'From our point of view the major difficulty was the cost. The only way we could get in there was by air via Kenya, which was an astronomical expense. To make it at all feasible we could only stay there for two weeks or so, and even then, as supplies of food were limited and unreliable, we had to have most of our food shipped out from England. This led to a second difficulty, which was that no one could be sure when the migration would take place. There was very little information to be had, and all we knew for certain was that the kob might come at any time between late September and early December. All I could do was get in contact with some missionaries in Pibor, who told me the times of the migrations in recent years.

'The second problem was, as usual, with the bureaucratic set-up. We were planning to fly in aboard a Kenyan-registered aircraft, but the political uncertainty in the Sudan at that time meant that any aircraft was a security risk. We got over that hurdle, and then the Sudanese conservation people told us that we wouldn't be allowed to film any dead wildlife. The Ministry of Information told us – direct from the President – that we would not be allowed to film any naked people. As many Murle do their hunting naked and a few thousand kob are killed, this made things downright impossible for us. I had to persuade them that our long lenses would enable us to select our images and the lighting was such that the naked people would appear as silhouettes. Their main worry was that we were going to portray the Sudanese as primitive tribesmen with no clothes on brandishing spears and butchering animals, which is supposedly not done in civilised society: Western people wear clothes and don't kill animals. But the whole aim of this sequence as far as David Attenborough was concerned was to show how the Murle fitted into their own ecosystem, hunting for food and for no other reason.

'We almost didn't get there at all. I spent one week in Khartoum trying to get various permits. I got completely stuck with one official whom I had to go through to reach somebody senior. Every day I would go in, suggest that he got in touch with his superior and he would say yes, he would. I'd ask him to phone and he would say he would, and then we would both sit there for an hour at the desk with

Two Murle hunters wait with their spears (*RM/BBC Enterprises*)

a telephone on it before he would actually make the call. Sometimes we would wait all morning, because as far as he was concerned it should have been him who had thought of the idea. I got so frustrated that I even took in a bottle of whisky, thinking this might speed things up. It turned out that he didn't drink!

'We had to take one Sudanese security man with us, which was fortunate because he understood the local language. But when we eventually got to Pibor, the tribesmen would not let us film. Apparently a German film crew had been out there two years before and had not endeared themselves to the locals. They had zoomed up and down the river in a motorboat and flown around in an aircraft and generally made a nuisance of themselves. That particular year very few kob had been killed, and the Murle blamed it all on the Germans; they were very nearly speared. The tribesmen immediately saw us as being from the same mould and you don't argue with a thousand armed hunters. Luckily the local government official was on our side and persuaded the others that we weren't going to cause any disturbance.

'That German film was really the only one that had been shot of the kob migration. I had been over to Germany to look at it and found that it only showed individuals hunting and not the mass hunt. They had been unlucky that year with the migration. So we were the first people to film the mass hunt and the result is spectacular. The hunters come to Pibor from all around. Some camp overnight at the river junction, others walk in from Pibor town before dawn. Then they settle down on their haunches on the outer banks of the two rivers. On what appears to be a signal (though what it was I never found out) they stand up *en masse* and run into the water, crossing the river and disappearing into the bush. If any kob are trapped in the junction all hell breaks loose, with men shouting and running in all directions. If the kob run into the water this slows them down and they become much easier targets – hunters converge on them from both sides and spear them. Only the kob which stay in large groups have a chance of surviving. Although there were some excellent hunters, many of them are not very efficient, just throwing their spears and hoping for the best. Sometimes a hunter is speared by mistake.

'Most of the hunting was over by daybreak, which meant that filming took place in very poor light. Only sporadic hunting occurred afterwards, and this was difficult to film as the kob sought refuge in dense bush. The migration is a time of big celebrations for the tribe, and even the soldiers stationed there join in. Once I saw a platoon standing to attention on their morning parade when suddenly out from a nearby bush jumped a female kob. The soldiers saw it, dropped their rifles, grabbed their spears, charged after the kob, cornered it, speared it and then rushed back, picked up their rifles and stood to attention again.'

The filming of the kob migration used up not only a lot of patience and time, but also money from Andrew Neal's share of the budget, but he very properly judged it to be worth the attempt and was vindicated by the result. However, he still had to find the extra money from somewhere, which meant taking it from one of his other programmes. He calculated that the last in the series, 'New worlds', was going to be the cheapest to make because it was about Man himself and involved relatively little travel to remote areas. He would be able to save on that and come in under budget, using the surplus to finance the Sudan trip. This explanation simplifies matters somewhat, but it contains the gist of a producer's reasoning.

By robbing Peter to pay Paul, as it were, Richard Brock, Ned Kelly and Andrew Neal were able to finance expeditions to places where few cameramen had ever been which produced some stunning footage. Martin Saunders filmed an enthralling fencing match between two huge narwhals, 'marine unicorns', in Arctic Canada. Further north still, Hugh Miles consistently got closer to polar bears than any other film-maker has done in the wild. Adrian Warren and

Ready for action Flying Hugh Miles to a remote part of the Arctic was an expensive gamble, but it paid off

Getting there Some of the almost inaccessible spots which cameramen penetrated: (below) prehistoric paintings inside caves in the Sahara (*AN/BBC Enterprises*); (right) the canopy of the Amazon rainforest (*AW*)

American freelance cameraman Neil Rettig spent days rigging an aerial ropeway 200 feet up in a jungle in Ecuador so that they could take a breathtaking tracking shot across the top of the forest canopy. Andrew Neal and his crew footslogged to a mountain plateau in the Sahara Desert to film ancient rock paintings. Each of these projects took many months to set up and a lot of cash and determination to see through.

Other 'nuggets' were picked up surprisingly cheaply. Before the first script had even been completed, Ned Kelly was given the golden opportunity of taking berths aboard a Royal Navy ship which was sailing to the South Atlantic. It was a rare chance to reach such utterly remote spots as the inland wastes of Antarctica and the South Sandwich Islands and he grabbed it, even though he had no precise idea of how the resulting material would be used. Naval helicopters were put at the team's disposal, enabling them to shoot some superb film of ice floes, elephant seals and penguin colonies, though unfortunately it proved impossible to record the smell of 14 million penguins packed together on one small island! The fact that the crew was stuck in Port Stanley in the Falkland Islands over Christmas did little to take away their delight at gaining such valuable sequences.

(Left) A colony of 14 million penguins on the South Sandwich Islands could only be reached by helicopter; (below) on landing, Hugh Maynard prepares to film chinstrap penguins (*NK/BBC Enterprises*)

Where's my camera? A weightless Martin Saunders during the zero-gravity filming (*AW/BBC Enterprises*)

The startling sequence with which the programme 'The sky above' opens shows David Attenborough, after a brief introduction on the importance of gravity, slowly rising from the floor. This was filmed in a Boeing 707 belonging to the American space agency, NASA. It is specially fitted with a padded compartment and flies in stomach-churning parabolas to simulate weightlessness. It took Adrian Warren and the film crew three days of flying to capture just the right moments and cost the BBC not a penny. NASA was pleased to give them the space, and knew that it would be good for their public image.

But it was not always necessary to travel to some faraway spot or employ dramatic effects to produce a memorable moment. Ian Calvert, director of the programme on the northern forests, wanted to include a scene in which David Attenborough walked up to a black bear's den, looked inside and showed a female hibernating inside. This would be doubly interesting because the black bear actually gives birth to her cubs and suckles them while she is in hibernation. It presented a challenge to both cameraman and presenter: one had to overcome the problems of filming a black object inside a dark hole using the minimum of lighting, while the other had to stand for several minutes within arm's length of a creature which could well become angry at being so rudely disturbed. Ian Calvert got in touch with several experts on the bear, cherished in the United States as *Ursus americanus*:

'It became obvious that if this sequence was going to be feasible at all, it would have to be shot in an area where there were plenty of bears. We fixed on a part of northern Pennsylvania which had the highest black bear population in the whole country: the animals had been well protected here, and in fact some people thought that they had been too well protected, because there were too many of them. The area is very popular with New Yorkers, who have holiday cottages in the hills, and set up huge troughs in their back gardens full of food for the bears. It's almost the equivalent of a bird table, except that it's meant for bears!

'The main reason for selecting a place with so many bears was that we had a greater number to choose from. Like human beings, black bears vary widely in temperament: some are quite docile and others are ferocious if annoyed. For our filming we had to find a docile female that would allow us to come fairly close to herself and her cubs with lights and a camera and not make a fuss. I was greatly helped by Gary Alt, who works for the Pennsylvania Game Commission and is constantly monitoring the bear population. He puts radio collars on the bears which can be used to follow the movements of the animals throughout the year, and to find out which dens the bears are using for hibernation.

Ursus americanus Some black bears are friendly; some are not (*AD Brewer/Ardea Photographs*)

'In December of that year he knew the whereabouts of nearly 80 bears, and it was a question of narrowing down that number to one that we could safely film. The black bears hibernate in all sorts of places, and clearly we wanted to find one somewhere on the ground; we also needed to find one that was reasonably friendly. Bears are fairly sleepy when they are hibernating, but they have the ability to wake up quickly if there is a disturbance outside the den. They go through a standard routine of aggressive postures to scare off intruders. First they make a whimpering sound with their upper lip drawn back to show their teeth; then they slap the ground with their paws; finally they rush out at you. So you can gauge what state the bear's in by its behaviour.

'Eventually we found a nice peaceable bear and began our filming. Because of the potential hazard of the situation we had to be very careful with lights, using only a low-powered battery light instead of full camera lights. Gary held this, because he knew the bears best and could quickly halt the filming if the bear was likely to be dangerous. On the first day it poured with rain and the battery light packed up, so we had to chase round all the local television companies looking for a replacement. On the second day we filmed for two hours without a hitch before Gary saw the female's lip curling and said we had to stop. The cameraman Martin Patmore had just enough time to get clear before she started banging the ground with her paws and pushed her head out of the den. After a grumpy look around she went back inside. We got about 90 seconds of that in the programme, and as far as I am aware, it has never been shown on television before.'

A minute and a half from two hours of shooting is a fairly good return. Often the cameraman will have to wait much longer than that, especially when he is not concentrating on an animal as well-trained as David Attenborough. Filming a certain aspect of animal behaviour can be a humdrum business, entailing long hours of sitting in a cramped hide hoping for the requisite mating display or hunting manoeuvre. A cameraman's time costs money too, so the producer is likely to give him a fixed period in which to obtain his shots. Something of the common-or-garden routine of the lone cameraman can be found in this snatch from Neil Rettig's diary, written for his own information whilst filming the great grey owl in Canada.

24 Feb. 1983
At 5.00 a.m. Bob Nero arrived and we headed towards the great grey owl area near Roseau. We drove from 5.00 a.m. until 2.00 p.m. looking for owls from the car. After lunch we set out for the owl area again, driving in all about 200 miles – returned at 6.30 p.m. During

Feb 27th con't

Feb 27th con't
        it was in line with the trunk.
I panned up the tree somewhat slowly
stopping on the stationary bird. We
did several takes as well as a few
close-ups with the 500mm and shots with
the 300mm from a greater distance. The
bird took a shit and flew screen left -
this was with the 300mm lens exposed
between f. 8, 5.6. On the way back
through Roseau bog. There was a bird on
a pole and I exposed a number of
shots of it taking flight or already flying,
very late afternoon at 100 F.P.S.

Introduction pan/zoom to owl perched in popular forest pan Screen Right →	Med shot full frame of Bird	Big close-up of owls face
owl turns head suddenly	owl flys off of perch	150 F.P.S. owl in flight
VOLE cut-aways	owl plunges into snow	finishy VOLE

A great grey owl (*P. Morris/ Ardea Photographs*)

this time I exposed 180 feet on the Arriflex, mostly with the 650 mm lens. Head shots and side- and back-lit shots of the birds. On the Photosonic I exposed about 70 feet on one owl flying half out of frame; the rest on an owl perched.

25 Feb 1983

We woke at 6.30 a.m. and stayed out until 6.30 p.m. The day was sunny for the most part. We filmed quite a number of static shots of the owls – some back-lit as well as some with the sun fully on them. Also we filmed a few feet of a great horned owl hunting by day. Most of the birds along the road to Roseau were tagged with a large yellow marker and number: this made it difficult to take any shots of them.

26 Feb. 1983
We woke again at 6.30 a.m. The conditions were much better for finding owls. Overcast skies. During the day we saw seven birds, some of which gave moderate performances for the cameras. The first bird at 8.00 a.m. flew out of a tree and snatched a mouse. The camera speed was intended to be 100 FPS but only reached 24 FPS – my fault because of the double trigger on the Photosonic. This bird was moving camera screen left ← : I'm sure the shot will be two stops over. The next bird we saw gave us a nice portrait series – it was sitting in an aspen copse. Used the 500 mm lens, exposed a bit then moved in for a tighter shot. Next we found a third bird in the same area. I exposed most of one natural plunge at 100 FPS, then quite a nice attempt at a vole: the bird was flying at an oblique angle towards the camera, slightly to the left. I pulled zoom back and followed it in a circle back to the tree. Next we filmed a bird snatching a mouse – twice. This should look OK – in one case the head and shoulders filled the frame!

And here, in rather quainter English, is an extract from a letter written to Ned Kelly by Hans Hvide Bang, a freelance film-maker who was looking for snowy owls in Norway:
'On Sunday the 18th we went into the Abisko area by helicopter. The sunny warm weather had turned to cloudy and cold and so it lasted during the whole period of the filming. We were well equipped with food and clothes, so we were in no needs, except from a bit freezing during the most colding periods.

A snowy owl (*John Daniels/Ardea Photographs*)

'The snowy owl's nest were situated on the ridge of a small hill. When I visited it on the same Sunday I found five chicken (nestlings) in the nest. The two smallest ones were dead. Because rain and cold weather I didn't put up the hide that day. When I arrived next day the two dead chicken had been eaten up. I put up the hide at about 20 metres from the nest. When the owl had accepted it I slowly moved closer and ended up at a distance of 10 metre. When we first came to the nest both male and female owl were present. Later only the female showed up. In the first period the female stayed most of the time on the nest warming the chicken.

'I believe that most of the feeding took place during the night, when there was too dark for filming. Nevertheless my German dog Linn was clever to hunt lemming. I then placed those lemmings on rocks in the nest surroundings. It worked out, and thanks to the clever dog I got the shots from the owl bringing and feeding the chickens with lemming. I stayed in the hide eight to ten hours a day. During this period I only observed one time that the owl caught a lemming herself.'

It is dedicated men such as these who provide the bulk of material for the series. But they are entirely dependent upon the whims of the animals involved, upon accidents of weather and terrain, and upon luck generally. No animal is completely predictable in its behaviour, and a wild and free spirit such as a snowy owl is beyond the reach of human persuasion. Other animals, however, need no second bidding to perform in front of the camera. Indeed, some of them don't know when to stop, as Richard Matthews discovered when he borrowed a captive armadillo from a Brazilian zoo.

'It was the only giant armadillo in captivity in the whole world, and we were lucky enough to be able to borrow it for one night. The Zoo officials crated it up, which was no easy matter, because it weighed about 130 lb, was built like a tank and was incredibly powerful. The idea was to place it in a field near some termite mounds and film it digging into the mounds to eat the grubs. We took three wardens from the Zoo with us, found a nice field, pointed the crate towards some termite mounds and opened the door. We were all standing round in an arc to try and guide the animal in the right direction, hoping that it would smell the termites and get totally absorbed in digging them out. This armadillo only forages at night, so we had lights set up: we knew our specimen was hungry, because it hadn't eaten for a day. We dug some of his usual zoo food into the ground near the mound hoping he'd smell it and start digging.

'The armadillo ambled out of the crate, took one look at us, whipped round the corner and was off into the darkness. So there we were without an armadillo, the only one (until that moment) in a zoo in the whole world. We all tore after it into the bush, which wasn't easy as it was pitch black, and managed to grab hold of the animal, which wasn't easy either because it was very slippery, the shape of a torpedo and with very powerful front legs and hind legs. A hand caught amongst the paws could easily get ripped open, especially when the armadillo withdraws a leg back into its armour. Three of us caught hold of it by one leg, but it just kept on moving with no apparent effort. Eventually we got it back to the termite mound, but by this time it had lost all interest in eating; all it wanted to do was escape. After two hours of chasing this creature and hauling it back we were all exhausted. The Zoo officials suggested that we put a rope round its neck in order to stop it running away.

'The trouble then was that I couldn't get the rope off! Every time I tried to loosen it the armadillo would roll on to its back and attempt to claw me. I was getting terribly sorry for the poor animal, because all I wanted it to do was dig into a mound and all it wanted to do was charge off into the bush. In the end it started digging and I managed to slip the rope off with no difficulty, but the cameraman had to keep his shot in very close, otherwise he would have had me and about half-a-dozen other people in the frame. The next panic was that the armadillo wouldn't stop digging. Even at over four feet long they can disappear into the ground very quickly, whether the going is hard or soft. Once they get halfway in they can brace themselves against the sides and no force on Earth can pull them out again. This one was by now about halfway in and the people from the Zoo were going berserk, thinking that they could wave goodbye to their prize attraction. I told them that we had to wait until we had properly filmed the sequence, but they were distraught with wondering how they were going to break the news to their boss. Luckily I had foreseen the problem and had brought a 40-gallon drum of water along. We tipped this down the hole after the armadillo and he relaxed his grip to come up for air. This enabled us to grab him, and out he popped safe and sound. I think we all felt more exhausted than he did.'

Many people will be surprised – even outraged – to learn that the giant armadillo they saw on the screen for a few fleeting seconds, happily excavating a termite mound, was in fact fresh out of a zoo. But how do you film a nocturnal, solitary and rare animal, very seldom seen? All you need is a minute or two of film, so it's not feasible to have

A giant anteater This specimen was borrowed from a zoo specially for the filming of 'Seas of grass' (*RM/BBC Enterprises*)

The extraordinary flying snake, which spreads its ribs and 'swims' through the air (*BBC Bristol*)

a cameraman stalking the animal for weeks hoping for a shot. Even the zoologists studying the armadillo for years hardly ever see one and only detect its presence from excavations. Throughout the series and the world of wildlife filming generally, this is a widespread and often necessary way of obtaining pictures of animals cheaply and under more or less controlled conditions. The giant anteater seen earlier in the programme 'Seas of grass' was also in captivity, as were many of the reptiles in 'Jungle' and many of the rodents in 'The baking deserts'. The dramatic sequence of the flying snake seen in Adrian Warren's programme on jungles was partly shot by taking a specimen up to 300 feet, dropping it from a weather balloon at an airfield in Brunei and filming it as it fell (the snake took this in its stride and suffered no ill-effects). Nearly all close-up shots of insects, such as the pseudo-scorpions in the forest leaf litter and the grass-cutting ants in the pampas, were taken in a studio under specialised conditions.

Several of the creatures would have spent their whole life in captivity, far away from their natural habitat. In his programme on rivers, 'Sweet fresh water', Richard Brock wanted to show the extra-ordinary breeding behaviour of certain species of fish. The tropical discus fish, for example, has fry which feed on its flanks in clouds of 30 or 40. This had never been filmed, and the chances of getting a sequence in the fish's native tropics were nil. Richard Brock, in desperation, asked around the local pet shops in Bristol and was told of a man in Surrey who might be able to help. He kept discus fish in his garage, fetching fresh spring water nearly every day, and had created just the right conditions for them to breed and feed in the natural manner. This was a lucky chance, and Richard Brock and cameraman Ron Eastman went to film the fish immediately. Ironically enough, the owner of the discus made his living by mending fish-frying equipment!

Richard Brock was also on the trail of the splashing tetra. This fish lays its eggs out of the water by leaping up to an overhanging leaf, depositing the eggs and jumping back in again. It will do this many times until it has laid a couple of hundred eggs. Then the male splashes the eggs to keep them moist until they are hatched, knowing by some intuitive process how to look after something which he cannot even see. Specimens of the tetra were imported from the Amazon and placed in tanks, but steadfastly refused to splash. Then, through a specialist magazine, Richard Brock was put in touch with an old lady in the Portobello Road in London who had some fish which *were* splashing. The filming of these failed, but some well-behaved tetra were eventually borrowed from a lorry-driver in Loughborough and the desired shots were obtained by London Scientific Films a long way from the Amazon jungle.

It would be wrong to suggest that film taken under these controlled conditions – in tanks, laboratories and zoos – makes up more than a small proportion of the final programmes. But is even this degree of artificiality justified in a series which purports to show the natural world? Does it matter if a fish is jumping in Brazil or in London? Are these all just extremely clever tricks of the trade or are they instances of dishonest artificiality? David Attenborough, for one, has no doubts at all about the realities of modern wildlife filming:

'If you're making a film and saying to people "Look here, this is an adventure story. Here is a man going out into the jungle, hacking his way through the undergrowth, looking for a very rare animal and this is it", and then you put a shot of a captive animal at the end, then you are being dishonest. That is something I have never done and I would never defend it. But, if you are saying "Look here, this is a flying frog which has parachute skin between its feet that enables it to glide", then you are simply making a biological point about a frog flying. Now you will never get a shot of a frog flying if you sit in the jungle and wait for one to glide past – at least, if you did it would take an enormous amount of time and money and the conditions would not be very photogenic. So you have to find the frog instead and persuade it to fly. If it does it in the jungle that's fine, but if it does it in the Palm House at Kew Gardens that's just as good, because you are being faithful to the biological truth. If you took the same frog to the Arboretum at Kew, dropped it onto some pine needles and pointed out that it suffered pain when landing on pine needles, then you would be distorting the truth, because that frog would never live anywhere near coniferous trees.

'But, having said that, one has to remember that all documentary films are distortions of facts. You are distorting time, say, by turning a 3-week expedition into a 30-minute programme. All the viewer can do is to trust in the veracity and good faith of the man who is making the film. This series, for example, is about biological truth: it is *not* about D. Attenborough in his shorts flogging through the swamps.'

With *The Living Planet*, more than perhaps any other natural history series, the strand of biological truth has been hard to maintain intact. Whereas *Life on Earth* concentrated on different families of animals which could often be filmed without reference to their environment, the new series set out to examine entire ecosystems. This made it necessary to hop from continent to continent, from hemisphere to hemisphere and from mountain peak to ocean floor, all in the space of 55 minutes. David Attenborough is all too conscious of the fact that his lightning switches from Africa to South America and thence to Indonesia may strain the credulity of even the most gullible viewer, but sees it as an unavoidable element in such an ambitious undertaking.

The other threat to biological truth comes from lack of time and money. Many fish can only be satisfactorily filmed in a tank: they cannot escape from the camera, as they might do in a river, but otherwise their behaviour is not circumscribed. Sitting in a studio, the cameraman is saved the expense of finding the right stretch of river, locating the right specimens, setting up an underwater camera and waiting for an indeterminate length of time until the right piece of action occurs: the river water might be cloudy, the fish unco-operative and the conditions dangerous to the film-maker. Naturally, in such circumstances, it makes sense to use a studio. The lengths which are gone to in order to create exactly the right controlled atmosphere are eloquent proof that laboratory filming is far from being just a soft option.

Perhaps the only person to suffer from this concentration on specialised filming, whether in the wild or in the studio, is David Attenborough himself. As the presenter, he appears in a wide variety of more or less exotic locations, but often he is alone; the animals are being filmed elsewhere:

'The reason I like making natural history programmes is that I can spend time watching animals. In this kind of programme I actually spend very little time doing that: I think the cameramen have more fun making it than I do!'

TRAVELLERS' TALES
The right people in the right place
at the right time

As the techniques of wildlife filming have grown ever more sophisticated, so the itineraries involved have grown ever more complex and crowded. David Attenborough, who made the first of his famous *Zoo Quest* expeditions for the BBC in 1974, appreciates the irony of this:

'Thirty years ago, the cameraman and I would go off to, say, Borneo for four months. It took an awfully long time to get there, and nobody could ring you up in the middle of the jungle. After four months we would come back with enough material for six half-hour programmes. But now – necessarily and rightly – the sizes of the units are so much bigger and the technical standards that have to be kept up are so much greater that travel has become very expensive. You may have a team of five or six people going, so you have to have it all planned down to the last detail to make sure that nobody is sitting around idle. You whiz in, do the filming, and whiz out again.'

Throughout the three-and-a-half years that it took to make *The Living Planet* there was a great deal of whizzing of one kind or another. An eager BBC publicity copywriter calculated that David Attenborough alone travelled more than 150 000 miles in that time – the equivalent of six journeys round the world – and that the crews filmed in 63 out of the 157 countries of the world. What he failed to mention was that much of this travelling consisted of simply sitting in an airliner. The tedium of intercontinental travel would certainly have become unbearable to the crew (David Attenborough, for one, dislikes airport-hopping) had it not been for the exotic nature of the places they were bound for. Locations that would be too expensive and too remote to reach under ordinary circumstances were laid open for them: faraway islands in the balmy Pacific and in the inhospitable South Atlantic; the barren wastes of the Sahara Desert and of Antarctica; a Himalayan gorge and an Andean mountain plateau; tropical rainforests in Ecuador and mangrove swamps in Bangladesh; an underground lava tube in Hawaii and a high-altitude balloon four miles above the Earth's surface.

The unenviable task of plotting these expeditions falls mainly upon the shoulders of the producer's assistants and secretaries who may not even have the compensation of going on the trips themselves. Apart from the hard slog entailed in obtaining filming permission from all corners of the globe, they are responsible for logistical details big and small. Diana Richards, assistant to Andrew Neal, had learned a lot during her years with the Natural History Unit and was able to make use of her experience on the new series. Her personal check-list is methodically gone through when preparing for every trip, and covers (with subsequent additions) every contingency:

passports
supplementary passports
visas
vaccinations
foreign travel form
   daily rate
   rate of exchange
itinerary schedule
   hotels
   flights
   cars
check public holidays
credit cards
   hire cars
   telephone
   American Express
driving licence
   international?
contacts list
maps
books

notify overseas offices
book film crew
shipping lists
special clothing
technical requirements
film stock
additional passport photographs
excess baggage
copy of insurance details
budget

Things to take filming
permits
stopwatch
iron
typewriter
scripts
schedules
stationery
first aid
air tickets

money/travellers' cheques	filming permission
roll/shot numbers	walkie-talkies
location catering	diary
cassette recorder/tapes	expenses form
expenses forms	calculator
collect travellers' cheques etc.	binoculars

Neil Rettig checks his equipment in a Holiday Inn – a typical cameraman's habitat (*NR*)

The list gives some idea of the welter of paperwork in which a traveller can get engulfed, but without which he would not get very far. Besides the standard passport, all are advised to carry additional photographs of themselves, to be held in reserve in case a new document is needed. Some countries refuse to accept holders of Israeli passports, others turn away South Africans, and so on. The issuing of visas often depends on convincing the relevant authorities that the filming will be beneficial to their country and that permission has been given by all the other departments involved. Fortunately the reputations of, respectively, *Life on Earth*, David Attenborough and the BBC Natural History Unit have tended to smooth the way. The worldwide success of *Life on Earth* was so great that the new series, following so swiftly on its heels, was able to take advantage of its popularity.

Equally vital are the various health certificates. The fate of an entire trip can hang upon these pieces of paper, as Hugh Maynard recalls with some feeling:

'Before going to Brazil we were each supposed to have been given a form by their London consultate confirming that we had all had the right injections and vaccinations. When we got to Manaus airport everybody else went through the barrier and there was I on the wrong side searching frantically through my pockets and insisting in a loud voice that I'd never been given the form. I was just wondering whether I was going to be deported when at last, in a final scrabble through my belongings, I found it.'

Every country has its own rules about which injections are required, and another of the assistant's crucial jobs is to find out exactly what is needed and then fix up appointments with the BBC nurse for every member of the party. Once she has pushed them through the routines of cholera jabs, yellow fever jabs and so on she has to try and persuade them to pack the optional extras, such as anti-malarial pills: these are not officially essential, but it would be a foolish traveller who left them behind. 'People don't like taking them much', says Diana Richards, 'David Attenborough thinks they'll make him blind! But I feel a personal responsibility for the health of the team. If anybody becomes ill on a trip it's of course his own fault, but ultimately it reflects back on to me.'

Once the basic itinerary has been decided on, the assistant works her way through the journey, booking air tickets, arranging connections, hiring cars and vans to take the crew and equipment to their locations, and booking hotel rooms. This last needs to be more carefully thought out than it might appear, because about 50 per cent of work abroad is done in hotel rooms: the cameraman has to clean his gear, unload his film and do his paperwork; the producer has to ring his contacts and make sure of his next day's filming; David Attenborough has to polish up his commentaries and fit any new material into his master file; the assistant has to type out the details of the day's work, and transcribe all recorded commentary. Ideally, the hotel management should be as amiable and sympathetic as possible, because they will have to put up with guests who keep odd hours, are usually tired, often encrusted with mud and dust and always encumbered with mountains of valuable equipment.

The Best A-Komodation in Town! The island of Komodo boasts only one ferry (above) and one hotel (below) (*NK*)

If most of their travelling has been done in the clinical no-man's-land of jet airliners, the crews have also had to clamber in and out of an extraordinary variety of vehicles, including helicopters, hot-air balloons, skidoos, sailing boats, hang-gliders, float planes and dug-out canoes. Clamber was often the operative word, as Marney Shears discovered in Indonesia:

'To get aboard the ferry boat which was taking us to Komodo, we had to paddle out a few yards into the water, squeeze ourselves somehow into a dug-out canoe, balancing all our gear on our laps, and wait to be rowed out to the boat. The you simply have to scramble up a network of ropes and tyres onto the deck. I was dreading it, but sheer panic got me up: I wasn't going to fail in front of the rest of the crew!'

Indonesia also boasted a highly idiosyncratic kind of six-seater coach,

Resolute
**Arctic Ocean, ice,
white whales**

Arctic Circle

Iceland
volcano

Scotland
balloon

England
various

Newfoundland
ocean

Washington
Mt.St.Helens

Chicago
**world's
tallest building**

Pennsylvania
black bears

California
Death Valley

Arizona
**cactus
desert**

Oklahoma
tornadoes

Carolina
forest fire

Texas
NASA, zero gravity

Tropic of Cancer

Hawaii
**lava tubes and
fruit flies**

Tassili
**rock paintings
desert**

Equator

Ecuador
**Waorani Indians
and volcano**

Peru
**guano, ducks
and *Amazon***

Brazil
**waterlily, grasslands
and *Amazon***

Tropic of Capricorn

Antarctic Circle

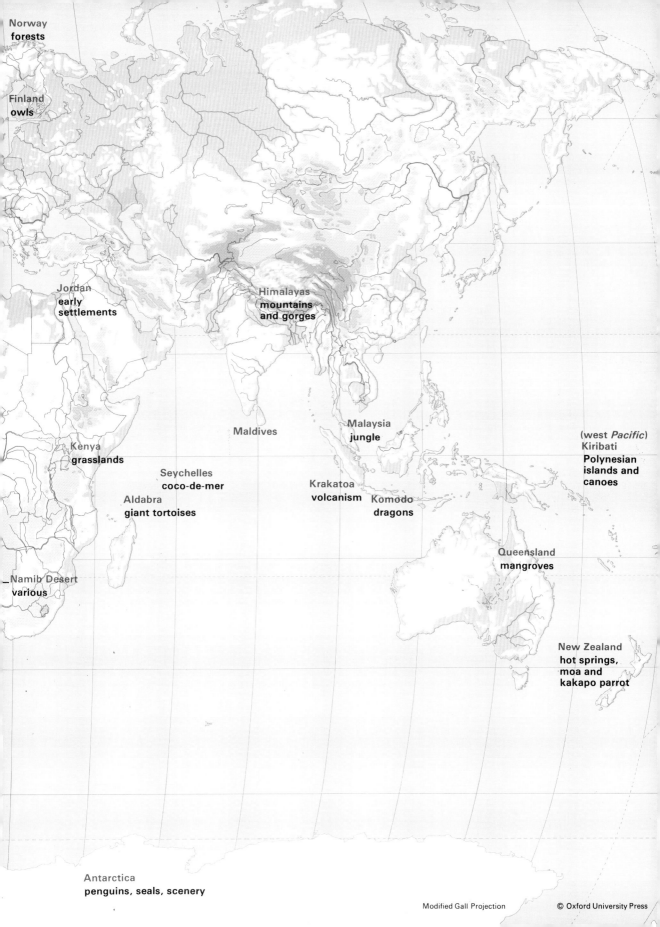

Norway
forests

Finland
owls

Jordan
early
settlements

Himalayas
mountains
and gorges

Kenya
grasslands

Maldives

Malaysia
jungle

(west *Pacific*)
Kiribati
Polynesian
islands and
canoes

Seychelles
coco-de-mer

Aldabra
giant tortoises

Krakatoa
volcanism

Komodo
dragons

Queensland
mangroves

Namib Desert
various

New Zealand
hot springs,
moa and
kakapo parrot

Antarctica
penguins, seals, scenery

Modified Gall Projection   © Oxford University Press

Location catering Diana Richards with today's menu in the Kalahari Desert (*Diana Richards*)

which had decorated ceilings and soft red interior lighting. As a final luxurious touch, the foot brake operated a musical tape so that every time the coach slowed for a bend the passengers were treated to a snatch from 'Auld Lang Syne'. They needed something to take their minds off the driving, which was usually at 50 miles an hour along a narrow mountain road with a sheer drop on one side and a lorry looming up in the distance. It was not much comfort to have the more recent pieces of wreckage pointed out to them in the valley below, or to learn that no Indonesian drivers are insured.

Booking air tickets, hotel rooms and transport is not always enough; sometimes, for trips to remoter corners of the world, the food has to be bought as well. Richard Matthews, for instance, estimated that his expedition to the Southern Sudan was going to last for at least six weeks, and it was discovered at the eleventh hour that food supplies in that part of East Africa were virtually non-existent. All provisions, said the safari organisers, would have to be flown in from Switzerland – at a phenomenal cost. The only alternative (and a much cheaper one) was to buy all the food in Bristol and send it out as air freight via Kenya. Diana Richards was given only three days' notice, so she jotted down the numbers of people, meals and days involved and made some rapid, rough-and-ready calculations.

Then she dashed to the nearest cash-and-carry supermarket and ran-sacked the shelves to the tune of four hundred and three pounds and tuppence. Nineteen boxes were filled with everything from tinned casserole to toilet rolls, by way of bread mix, long-life milk, egg powder, porridge oats, Kendal mint cake, tomato ketchup, soap powder and tea towels. There was even a birthday cake for Richard Matthews, converted lovingly from a tinned Christmas cake with the aid of a few candles. Finally, the indefatigable Mrs Richards typed up a menu with suggestions as to what should be eaten in which order.

Like a mother hen, the producer's assistant has to chivvy her brood along and provide them with the answers to a hundred questions, most of which they will not think to ask. What will the weather be like when they arrive? What sort of clothes should they wear? What is the time difference? When are the shops open? What sort of driving licence is needed? What is the local electric current? What is the rate of exchange? All these, plus the flight timetable, rendezvous points and other travel details eventually cohere into the crew's lifeline – the schedule. This is a fairly random process, as Beth Huntley explains: 'Once I've got too much information to hold in my head I type it out, and that becomes the basic schedule.'

The schedule will be added to, knocked about, torn up and re-typed several times before it emerges as the final and definitive document. Perhaps the most intricate and wide-ranging of these was the 28-page monster prepared by Marney Shears for Ned Kelly's trip around the world in 1982. This marathon began with four of the party flying from Gatwick airport to Indonesia. There they met Ian Calvert, who had been travelling round the globe the opposite way in order to make all the arrangements (as he hoped) in advance, and later David Attenborough and Dicky Bird. Next they sailed to Krakatoa, returned to Jakarta and flew on to Bali. Although 24 September was a Friday ('Muslim Religion – Fridays are Days Off – Dress Should Be Sober and Behaviour Restrained!' warned the schedule), they still managed to make the perilous sea crossing to the island of Komodo. Next stop was Sydney, Australia, followed by Auckland, New Zealand and a flight down the whole length of North and South Islands and back. The most uncertain section of the journey came next, island hops on ever-tinier private airlines to the scattered Kiribati Islands in mid-Pacific. There was only one airfield in the whole group, and from there the party had to travel by light plane, missionary truck and canoe. They then had a single day to do their filming before the whole convoluted procedure had to be performed in reverse. If one part of the arrangements had failed, they might have been stuck there for another month. As it was, they hurried on to Honolulu and, eventually, home.

A dot in the schedules Airlines on Pacific Islands such as Kiribati are not only limited but often erratic too (*NK*)

(Previous page) Some of the many forms of transport used in filming *The Living Planet*: hot-air balloon, twin-engined aircraft, dug-out canoe, sea plane, buffalo, jeep, skiddoo (and trailer), sailing boat, helicopter, native porters (*AW, NR RB, RM, Andrew Neal*)

(Opposite page) **Travelling heavy**   Film crew and equipment at Brunei Airport (*NR*)

It is easy enough to pick up a telephone and speak to a travel agent who can fix you tickets to the international airports of the world. But what do you do if an airline has no telephone number, no agents and no booking office? Marney Shears managed to book flights with the miniscule operators in the Gilbert Islands by simply bombarding them with cables and telex messages; these took ten days to arrive and there was another wait for ten days before an answer came back. Beth Huntley had even greater difficulties when she tried to arrange an expedition to the Maldive Islands in the Indian Ocean:

'We first of all had to find out who the Maldives actually belonged to, so we rang up the Sri Lankan embassy in London. They said that the islands had their own government but had no representative in Britain. There were few telephones there and, as far as we knew, no telex receivers, so we just had to write a letter introducing ourselves and saying that we were coming! We got no reply, which just goes to show that you should always aim for countries that have a good telephone system.'

The cost of travel for a six-man team is expensive enough, but it pales into insignificance when set beside the value of the technical equipment involved. A single camera is worth more than £10 000, and when lenses, camera magazine, tripod and other necessaries are included, the total soars to nearly £30 000. Add to that another £3000 for sound equipment and the final figure comes to something like one per cent of the entire budget for the series. The problem with this is neither the purchase price (they are BBC property) nor the cost of insurance (handled by BBC Shipping), but the recurrent headache of customs controls. Strictly speaking customs duty is payable on all the equipment when it enters a country, and can be reclaimed when that equipment is taken out of the country again. To bypass this cumbersome system, many nations have entered into an international Carnet agreement under which the value of the duty is guaranteed and no money actually changes hands. The cameraman simply compiles a detailed list of all his gear, showing the serial numbers, country of origin and approximate value. This is stamped on entering and on leaving a foreign country, thus bringing bureacracy down to a minimum and wasting everyone's time as little as possible. It is the equipment's passport.

However, when a country is not party to the Carnet agreement, matters become considerably more tiresome. The BBC has to place a bond equivalent to the value of the duty in a local bank, usually entrusting a local agent on the spot to do it for them. When the film crew arrives at the customs barrier the agent is there to meet them

with the necessary certificate to prove that the money is sitting in a bank. When they leave again, the customs officer must stamp the document to show that the equipment has been taken out of the country, and the BBC can then reclaim its bond. If the documents are not properly filled in and stamped, then they won't get their money back. It is worth remembering that the BBC runs more than a hundred film crews altogether, and that the total value of their equipment comes to more than £2 million. At large airports the procedure works efficiently enough, but at a smaller and more remote establishment the chances are that the local customs officers will not understand how it works and will never even have set eyes on a carnet or a bond certificate. In this situation the cameraman can only explain matters politely without appearing to tell them what their job is.

Cameramen and sound recordists tend to have a very possessive attitude towards their equipment, and are reluctant to surrender it to the tender care of airline porters, so most of the time they will carry it themselves. As the number of cases can be anything from 3 to more than 20, this means that everyone in the party has to carry something. It also means that the gear is often classified as excess accompanied baggage, which is an expensive luxury but at least gives everyone peace of mind. If a cameraman can see and handle every case he will be less worried about having left something vital behind. The cheapest way is to send the equipment by air freight to an agent in advance, but this can only be done when there is a lot of time to spare. Gear that goes astray can hold up the filming and that, in the end, costs far more than the certainty of excess baggage. Martin Saunders has a particularly grim memory of this sort of disaster.

'Each individual country has its own laws and regulations about cargo and customs. We had planned a trip to Indonesia, and because we had a few weeks to spare we thought we would ship the equipment out by air freight. This turned out to be an absolute waste of time. We arrived with ten days to do our filming in, and I spent five of them trying to retrieve my cameras which had been impounded. All impounded goods were stored in vast sheds at the airport, and the first difficult job was actually to find out where they had put my gear. Every morning I would go along and hammer away at the Customs people, starting off with the bottom man, then being passed to his superior and so on up the line. The sheds were piled high with stuff and there are dozens of people clambering about looking for their belongings. The five days we lost there easily cancelled out the advantage of saving on excess baggage charges.'

The movement of baggage becomes an even greater problem when

main roads and airports are left behind, and the crew has to make its way more or less independently. Often a helicopter or canoe may be so small that it will have to make three or four trips, ferrying passengers and cases to the shooting location. This, too, can become expensive and individual initiative can save a lot of time and money, as Martin Saunders describes:

A Twin Otter aircraft Essential transport for Hugh Miles and his gear in the Canadian Arctic (*NK*)

'Travel around the Arctic is enormously expensive, because all the fuel has to be shipped long distances. When we were filming narwhals on Baffin Island, my assistant and I had to think of some way of getting ourselves and all our equipment to a tiny camp on the north coast, and the only way we could do it was by air. This would have meant a shuttle service by helicopter which would have cost us a fortune. So, on our way to the stopover point in the plane – a Twin Otter – I asked the pilot if he could fly out to the camp and maybe try landing there, just to see if it was feasible. The plane had special balloon tyres for landing in snow and rough ground so he agreed. He did a few circuits of the airstrip, which looked the size of a postage stamp with a cliff on one side and a sheer drop into the sea on the other. Then he came in at about 100 mph, 15 feet above the ground to check the surface of the runway, seemed satisfied and said he would give it a go. When we landed, people ran out from the camp and told us that it was impossible to land a Twin Otter there!

'We were lucky, of course, to have had such a good pilot, but we had saved quite a few pounds because we'd got everything delivered out there in one trip. After we had completed our shooting, the time came when we had to get ourselves out of there again. To save expense in the same way, obviously I tried to find another Twin Otter and another willing pilot. Eventually I contacted someone on the radio who jumped straight away into a helicopter, flew over and had a look at the runway. He said he was prepared to do it but only if some repair work was done to the strip first. He walked along it, pointing out where boulders would have to be moved and ditches filled in, and then flew off again. That evening we recruited a couple of the scientists at the camp, took picks and shovels out on to the runway and smoothed it all out. Next day the plane landed with no trouble and took us out in one go.'

No trip ever goes exactly according to plan: the schedule depends on too many variables for that. However, there are times when the variables can be so erratic as to put not only the details of the schedule but the lives of the film crew themselves in danger. The most dramatic instance of this occurred when Ned Kelly, with David Attenborough, Martin Saunders and Dicky Bird, hired a boat in the Seychelles to take them to the remote island of Aldabra, 700 miles to the south-west in the Indian Ocean. Here they hoped to film the giant tortoises which somehow lived on the inhospitable lump of coral. They chartered a trading yacht called *La Feline*, skippered by a Seychellois who seemed to know what he was doing. Here is Ned Kelly's tight-lipped diary of the next few days:

Sunday 6 Sept.
16.15 hours boarded the yacht *La Feline*.

The trading yacht *La Feline*
(*NK/BBC Enterprises*)

Monday 7 Sept.
5.30 a.m. Departed Mahé. During day seas became rougher making eating almost impossible as no non-slip mats available and highly polished dining table is without partitions.

Tuesday 8 Sept.
Unscheduled stop for three-and-a-half hours off Alphonse Island. Seemed unnecessary as meal was not served until we moved off into rough seas again. Rain later this day leaking through port side of cabins and through deck lights wetting the bunks of four passengers. This persisted throughout the voyage. Also 14 crew and passengers were having to share one bathroom/toilet.

Wednesday 9 Sept.
7.00 a.m. Running down the 'wrong' side of Providence Reef: navigational error. This meant our turning and retracing our course north before we could head west to Aldabra. Estimated time lost – four hours. Headed for St Pierre when engine broke down. Estimated time lost – three hours. Once engine restarted Captain gave ETA Aldabra as 13.00 hours Thursday 10th.

Thursday 10 Sept.
Captain said an island spotted on radar at 02.30 hours: he assumed this was Cosmoledo, therefore ETA Aldabra now 11.00 hours. At 09.00 hours and 11.00 hours radio calls were made to Aldabra in the belief that they were listening out for us: no reply to our calls. This was not surprising since the Research Station frequency was not amongst those obtainable through the crystals carried aboard *La Feline*. This station frequency could easily have been checked before our departure from Mahé. By 13.00 hours no sign of Aldabra. We queried his exact position and Captain then revealed that we were lost. Without a log he had guessed our speed to be 12 knots in which case we were now well past where Aldabra should have been. I asked the Captain if he had taken a sun-sight and he said 'It wasn't a very good one.' At 14.00 hours the yacht was turned round and headed back in an ESE direction. At 15.15 hours we convened a meeting to discuss the seriousness of the situation. The Captain was requested to take the opportunity of taking another sun-sight at 16.00 hours which would be our only chance of fixing our position before dark. He then said that he was only able to take them at noon and requested that our cameraman, who knew a little about navigation, should proceed with the sun-sight. A book was then produced called *Astro navigation for beginners* and we began to work through the complex mathematics necessary – this was made extremely difficult as the only Almanac on board was for 1980! Darkness fell with our position still not known.

Friday 11 Sept.
Woken at 06.00 hours with news that Aldabra had been found on the radar screen during the night and that we were now approaching land. At 06.45 hours it became apparent that this island was *not* Aldabra. Luckily one of the seamen was able to identify it as Cosmoledo, some 75 miles to the east of Aldabra. At 07.10 hours turned and headed for Aldabra and reached the anchorage off the settlement at 15.00 hours. Delays en route totalled approximately 34 hours.

Saturday 12 Sept.
Informed by Captain that the engine had broken down again. *La Feline* unable to return to Mahé to collect our colleague Ian Calvert as per the charter agreement.
That they arrived at all, when the next nearest land masses were either East Africa or Australia, was due to the perseverance and rudimentary sailing knowledge of Martin Saunders, who had done a little dinghy navigation in the past. David Attenborough had been in the Royal Navy during his National Service but his memories of

navigation were by now rather rusty. By puzzling their way through *Astro navigation for beginners*, the book discovered on the bridge, the pair managed to head the craft in the right direction, though they were further hampered by the fact that the Captain did not possess an accurate watch and the only general map they could find was a British Airways flight map of the Indian Ocean. 'We worked out how much water and beer we had left', remembers Dicky Bird, 'and eventually we decided that if we hadn't found our position after a few days we would head for East Africa and hope for the best.'

The research station on Aldabra (top) is a strictly temporary affair, but the giant tortoises are long-term inhabitants, managing to scrape a living somehow from the barren coral landscape (*NK/BBC Enterprises*)

Although they were a day and a half behind schedule when they landed on Aldabra, the crew were able to get down to filming straight away. The island itself is no fertile paradise but a coral rock heaved out of the sea and scoured by the winds and waves. Not much lives upon this jagged and barren terrain except some spiky bushes, seabirds and 150 000 giant tortoises, descended from a few which are thought to have drifted there on the current from Madagascar. With no predators, their numbers have increased enormously and now their problem is shortage of food. Not only do they turn cannibal if given the chance, they will also eat anything else going – including a stack of paint cans left outside the research station on the island. The sharp rocks made movement difficult for the BBC crew, but shooting went ahead satisfactorily. All that remained was the small problem of the broken-down *La Feline*.

Tortoise-eye view Martin Saunders getting down to his job on Aldabra (*NK/BBC Enterprises*)

Meanwhile Ian Calvert, blissfully unaware of those in peril on the sea, had arrived on schedule in Mahé. He planned to do a little research and setting up of locations while waiting for *La Feline* to return and ferry him to Aldabra. But he had barely checked in at his hotel before a frantic phone call from Ned Kelly came over the radio link (the island link with Aldabra operated for only one hour a day) telling him of the disaster. Ian immediately shot round to the charter company to sort out some means of rescue. It appeared that there were no other boats in the Seychelles available for hire, and that if *La Feline* was not repaired quickly, the crew could be stuck out there for anything up to a month.

'First of all we had to ascertain from Ned precisely what had gone wrong with the boat, which meant that they had to strip down the engine and locate the faulty part. Ned then had to describe the part to me over the crackling radio link and somehow from his verbal description we had to identify it in the relevant catalogue – which, thank God, I had managed to find at a local boat merchant's. Once we had decided on it, I discovered a boat in the harbour which had a similar engine to *La Feline* and persuaded the owner to sell me the requisite part. But however was I going to get it out to Aldabra? I got in touch with the Seychelles Air Force, which consists of a little monoplane which has been souped up by putting petrol tanks on the

(Above) Tea-time for the crew on Aldabra (*NK/BBC Enterprises*)
(Below) A robber crab still searching for his meal (*NK/BBC Enterprises*)

wings and is used for patrolling the fishery zones. Aldabra is right at the limit of its fuel range: the pilot could just about manage to fly out there, drop the part and fly back again before running out. So, he very kindly agreed to do the run and parachute the part down to the island.

'Satisfied that I had done all I could, I went off to make a recce of several locations round the islands. When I came back three days later I found that Ned had been making more desperate phone calls to say that the part had arrived all right but that it was the wrong one! I checked the catalogue again and couldn't see where I had made a mistake. The description that he had given me seemed to be correct, so I got in touch with the manufacturers in Britain, who told me that there was actually a printing error in the catalogue! The part I had identified had been given the wrong number. It was then a question of having the right part flown out from a warehouse back home: Diana Richards had to organise this and, with good luck for once, it arrived in Mahé only 48 hours later.

'The next problem was how to get it out to Aldabra. By that time I had asked around and found out that every boat capable of going as far as the island was already chartered, and that none would be free for at least a month. The Fisheries aircraft wasn't available either, and my last chance was the Seychelles Navy. This consisted of a motor torpedo boat and an old French minesweeper called the *Topaz*. It so happened that the *Topaz* was about to leave on a voyage to Tanzania taking some troops home who had been on exercise in the Seychelles. I looked at the map and worked out that it would only need a small detour from its course to call at Aldabra. By a stroke of luck we also discovered that the owner of our charter company had a cousin who was married to someone influential in the Seychelles government, and they arranged the diversion, with passage for myself and an engineer. We were very grateful, but it was not a very pleasant voyage. There must have been nearly 300 soldiers on board a boat that was equipped for 20. Everyone slept on deck and the soldiers spent most of their time being sick.'

Friday 25 Sept.
Our colleague Ian Calvert arrived on Aldabra aboard the military vessel *Topaz*, courtesy of the government of the Seychelles; with him were the spare engine parts which the BBC expedited from England. Engine of *La Feline* repaired and we departed on schedule at 16.30 hours.

They were actually four hours behind schedule, which was a remarkably short delay considering the complications. It could easily have been four months instead. However, the journey back was by no means trouble-free:

Saturday 26 Sept.
Took different route back. Headed NE for the Amirantes. The newly fitted log was lost at some stage during this day. Once again no definite knowledge of our position.

Sunday 27 Sept.
Our destination (landfall) is to be Daros. By afternoon this changed to Poivre. As darkness fell we made identifiable landfall on – *Daros*! Course far enough out to make everyone nervous again.

Monday 28 Sept.
Landfall on Silhouette Island and arrival Bird Island at 13.30 hours. Went ashore to film.

Tuesday 29 Sept.
After filming left Bird at 11.30 hours. Lunch on board. Reached Cousin at 16.00 hours. Made contact with wardens then sailed for Praslin for overnight anchorage. Went ashore for meal (at Captain's invitation).

Wednesday 30 Sept.
Sailed for Curieuse. Outboard motor for Zodiac ceased to work which meant ferrying people to and fro by rowing – lost us about two hours filming time on Curieuse. Returned to Praslin, lunch on board. Boarded bus for Vallée de Mai. Returned about 18.00 hours to find that Captain would like us all to go to La Digue that night for a meal. Our schedule will still be adhered to.

Clearly, the Captain was feeling some remorse for his own, and the boat's, shortcomings. At any rate, Dicky Bird never carried out his threat of 'making him walk the plank'. And they finished two days early!

Aldabra's birds (Left, top to bottom) heron, finch, green heron, (above) sacred ibis (*NK/BBC Enterprises*)

ON LOCATION
The work of the BBC film crews

The full film crew which accompanies David Attenborough is fondly known as the 'Circus' – a nickname derived from Barnum and Bailey rather than George Smiley. Each trip presents the members with a different set of requirements and problems. Once the cameraman and sound recordist know where they are going and what is expected of them, they can begin to select and pack their equipment. The cameraman has to decide whether to use a special 'sync' camera, which is noiseless and will thus avoid disturbance to the sound track, or the sturdier machine which is sometimes used for 'mute' filming. He take as big a range of lenses as the weight stipulations allow – wide-angles up to 5.9 mm (virtually a fish-eye), telephotos for taking close-up shots of subjects a considerable distance away, and the 'work horse', the zoom lens. Two types of film stock are usually carried, one for exposure in normal or bright daylight, and a faster film for dimmer conditions.

But the line has to be drawn somewhere. If a cameraman were allowed to bring every piece of equipment that he might need, an army of porters would have to be recruited just to carry the baggage. As it is, anyone with a spare hand is likely to have a tripod or camera case put into it. David Attenborough is greatly loved by film crews for his habit of seizing on the heaviest and most awkward item of luggage and striding off with it. Everything, therefore, is pared down to the very minimum – including the personnel – and the producer depends largely on the expertise and experience of his team for advice. Martin Saunders recalls one occasion where this came in handy:

'If I consider that something is going to be ridiculously expensive, then I shall point it out to the producer. For example, we were planning a trip to Malaysia to film leatherback turtles laying their eggs on a beach: this invariably happens at night and so artificial lighting is essential. But you can't go hauling a battery of lights and a lighting assistant halfway round the world just for one short sequence of film – it's not as if this was Hollywood! The producer and I asked the unit manager to find out if there were any lighting hire firms in Kuala Lumpur, which was the nearest big city to our location. As it turned out, there was one and the trip went ahead using their equipment, but in some remoter spot we might not have been so lucky and might have had to bear the expense of the extra staff and baggage. It's up to the producer to weigh up in his mind whether it is worth spending that much money in order to obtain that particular footage.

When you hire equipment and staff at such a long distance you're not going to know who will be working with you until you get there, which can make you slightly apprehensive. This was especially true

Big but elusive A leatherback turtle, found after a long search on a Malaysian beach (*Andrew Neal*)

of the Malaysian trip, because leatherback turtles are very easily disturbed. They emerge on the beach in the middle of the night, and if you start dazzling them with light and noise before they start laying their eggs they will simply turn round and disappear into the sea again. Once they are laying they are much happier and will accept the sudden brightness, so the switching on of the equipment has to be timed very accurately.

We had to make sure that the local lighting crew fully understood the delicacy of the situation, and work out an efficient early warning system for finding turtles that were actually laying. In the end we were helped by a team of Malays who ran up and down the vast length of beach looking for specimens. The film crew, plus David, were strategically placed somewhere in the middle, packed in a vehicle and ready for instant action if we heard a shout. Originally we set aside two nights to get the sequence we wanted, but not a turtle was sighted in that time. On the third night it bucketed down with rain. Finally, at about 3 o'clock on the fourth night, we were told that there were two turtles, one at each end of the beach. We were in a bit of a dither about which one to choose, but the driver took it upon himself to make a decision, and it was the right one, thank goodness.'

The sound recordist tends to be less heavily encumbered with equipment than the cameraman. A recorder filled with tape weighs about 25 lb, and is easily the bulkiest item he has to carry. The wide variety of microphones used – ranging from tiny radio mikes that can be clipped to a shirt-front to bigger devices which can be used to pick up a more general area of sound, such as a breeding colony of seabirds – can easily be fitted into one padded case, whilst the recorder goes into another. These, together with spares and replacement batteries and, if all else fails, a miniature recorder which can be slipped into a pocket, are the sum total of the sound man's requirements. As he will be called upon mainly to record the narrator in front of the camera, there is no need for awkward items such as booms.

Lyndon 'Dicky' Bird has been the companion of David Attenborough on almost every one of his sync filming trips, not only for *The Living Planet*, but for *Life on Earth* as well. Having comparatively little gear to worry about, he is a self-contained unit, carrying everything that he needs in a rucksack on his back. Sound recordists, like cameramen, are possessive about their hardware, and Dicky Bird's rueful philosophy is: 'Carry it yourself and you don't have to rely on other people to drop it for you.' One of his major worries is his stock of batteries. The intense cold of such places as the Antarctic

Sound man The indefatigable Dicky Bird recorded sound for the series under conditions which ranged from desert heat to icy cold (*RM, Andrew Neal*)

The Maldive Islands in the Indian Ocean (right) look idyllic enough, but beneath the surface lurk hungry sharks. (Below) Dicky Bird wires David Attenborough for sound before his dive (*RB*)

cuts the working life of a battery by a considerable percentage, and plenty of spares must be included. Nor can he rely on local traders for adequate replacements: in Africa and South America the only batteries available in shops are cheap and low quality ones, useless for the rugged job they have to do.

The making of *The Living Planet* was such an extraordinarily ambitious project that the film crews were forced to improvise and cover much new ground. When, for instance, David Attenborough was to be filmed swimming amongst sharks off the Maldive Islands in the Indian Ocean, Dicky Bird was asked to solve a singular problem.

On the sea bed David Attenborough speaks his piece to the camera (*RB*). (below) Hugh Maynard films two large reef sharks (*BBC Bristol*)

'No one had done much synchronised filming underwater before, at least not with any success. For this sequence we wanted to show that David was really doing the talking, to prove that his words hadn't been dubbed on afterwards. This meant starting from scratch. I got together with one of the engineers from the BBC workshops in Bristol, and we first of all designed a waterprooof housing for the small tape recorder which David could wear on his belt. Then we got hold of a full face mask through which you would be able to see the whole of his face, and taped a tiny microphone inside, connected to the recorder with wires running up underneath his diving suit. The microphone has to be one which would operate underwater despite the differences in pressure that you experience down there.

'Off we flew to the Maldives with this Heath-Robinson affair. David had been on a refresher course in diving at a special school in Plymouth. At the same time Hugh Maynard had gone down to test the new underwater housing for his camera. The results were inconclusive, because the water in the school's tank was so cloudy that Hugh couldn't see David even when they were touching each other! Once we got on location near the islands I dived down with David to test the recorder, but while the filming was on I stayed up on the surface with the producer, Richard Brock. The sharks were reported to be so tame that they could be fed by hand ("Whose hand?" asked Richard) but the presence of too many people might have upset them. Everything went according to plan, but when we got back in the boat I discovered that water had somehow seeped into the recorder. Sea-water can do a lot of damage to electrical equipment, so I quickly had to strip it down, wash it in fresh water and dry the parts off with a hair-dryer – and I'm not saying who that belonged to!'

Members of a film crew have two recurrent nightmares: one is that their equipment is going to break down irreparably in some remote spot; the other is that they are going to lose or leave behind some vital piece of gear. The first fear can be allayed somewhat by having everything rigorously overhauled before departure by the maintenance engineers. Then, as soon as that particular trip is over, the equipment is taken into the workshops again to be cleaned of all the dust, sand, salt and moisture that will have accumulated in its delicate insides. The second fear is less lingering. Once the cameras, lenses and so on have been securely packed in their strong metal cases, there can be a pile of anything from 3 to more than 20 separate pieces of baggage. The cases are tough enough to withstand the general airline staff's practice of dropping things from a great height on to tarmac, but will any of them get left behind? Everyone double-checks their cases, because they know that if anything is forgotten, it will be virtually impossible to ship out a replacement in time. 'Sometimes it's quite a relief to get on the plane', admits Martin Saunders, 'because once you are there it's too late to worry any more.'

On location these misgivings gradually disappear as the crew concentrates on the job of filming. The producer will already have a detailed shooting schedule and, together with the cameraman and sound recordist, he will visit the location a day before the rest of the party to choose the exact sites for placing the camera. These depend on a whole host of imponderables: the background must be carefully considered; there must be enough space for zoom or tracking shots,

Martin Saunders relaxes during the flight, hoping that all his equipment is safe in the hold (*Dicky Bird/Diana Richards*)

On land again, he often has to carry most of it himself (*AW*)

which will show David Attenborough as part of the scenery, rather than just the focus of it; the cameraman will want to find out when the light is at its best (usually this is in the morning) and the sound recordist will want to discover if there are going to be any problems from wind noise, nearby roads or aircraft activity.

Next morning, the whole crew goes to the location and the equipment is set up. David Attenborough is usually wired for sound by having a small radio microphone clipped unobtrusively on his clothing, but make-up is not an important consideration for him. Each piece will probably begin with a developing shot of the narrator walking into the foreground, stopping and speaking his commentary exactly on cue. The text for this will have been written and learned, and at least one rehearsal will be made without the camera running. Then comes the decisive moment – the first take. Camera and tape recorder roll, David Attenborough walks and talks, and everyone else holds their breath. Sometimes this take is the best, but by some unfortunate coincidence, motorbikes and aircraft may choose the same moment to pass by; the sun disappears behind a cloud; a bird flies out of a tree, distracting the viewer's attention.

One item not needed is a cue board for David Attenborough: he learns his lines thoroughly (*RM*)

So the whole thing has to be run again. The unofficial formula is: one take for the cameraman, one for the sound man, and one for the producer. There may even have to be one for Attenborough himself, although as a vastly experienced broadcaster he rarely fluffs his lines. He may decide to do it again simply in order to change the emphasis on certain words in the commentary. On one unforgettable occasion he had to speak his piece while standing on a steep ice slope. He had just finished speaking to the camera when his legs slipped from under him and he unceremoniously disappeared from shot, ending up chortling and unhurt 15 feet lower down.

However, there are plenty of less amusing interruptions to the shooting. It may happen that, after half-an-hour of careful preparation in brilliant sunshine, a cloudbank will appear and hold up shooting for another half-hour. Every cameraman has known the frustration of abandoning a day's filming because of poor light, packing up his gear and climbing into the vehicle, only to find that the sun has just poked its way out of the gloòm. The schedules are so tight that there is often no opportunity to return to that location for a second attempt. Of course even the most hardened professional is fallible, and Martin Saunders and Hugh Maynard will readily admit to the odd embarrassing blunder, such as jerking the camera when operating the zoom lens.

One of the secrets of David Attenborough's success as a communicator is his restless activity, a dislike of standing still for too long and becoming just another 'talking head'. This energetic enthusiasm is conveyed as he strides along mountain ridges, trudges up hills and stands ankle-deep in icy streams, emphasising each point with a pair of wonderfully expressive arms. It seems as if no kind of exertion – climbing ropes to the top of a giant kapok tree, struggling to suck oxygen from his mask in a balloon at 20 000 feet, being nudged by sharks in the Indian Ocean, floating around weightless in the belly of a jet aircraft – can quench his eagerness.

In the face of all this, it is easy to forget that the cameraman has to keep pace with him, holding a heavy camera on his shoulder. A tripod is fine for stationary work, but for much of the time it has to be discarded. Supporting the weight of a camera calls for a great deal of strength and stamina, but Martin Saunders firmly believes that the heavier it is the better:

'It all comes down to experience. If I have to film David walking towards the camera, obviously I have got to be walking backwards myself with the camera on my shoulder. To keep the picture smooth I have developed what I call "the cameraman's crouch", which involves bending the knees to give myself a sort of sprung suspension. In this way I can hold the top half of my body absolutely steady, and a heavy camera will give the best results because the sheer weight prevents me from jerking it. When I look through the lens I have to be very conscious of certain things. I check constantly that the picture is in focus, and watch the edges of the frame very carefully. If you are filming a moving object, then the very action of that thing moving will divert attention from any unsteadiness. But if you are filming something that is stationary, you can see quite clearly from the amount of movement at the edge of the frame if you are beginning to waver. It is impossible to get a completely steady picture with

Attenborough at large Catching insects in Sussex, (*Hugh Maynard, AW*), being baked in Death Valley (*Andrew Neal/BBC Enterprises*), hanging about in Venezuela (*Diana Richards/BBC Bristol*), dwarfed by cactus in Arizona (*Diana Richards/BBC Bristol*)

Action! The camera and tape recorder roll as David Attenborough is filmed on Krakatoa (*NK*)

a hand-held camera, but you have to try to cut it down to a minimum.

'It can be quite exhausting sometimes. One particularly gruelling episode was the filming of David with the mountain gorillas in Rwanda for the *Life on Earth* series. These creatures lived in very dense vegetation at an altitude of about 10 000 feet, and in order to get near them we had to obey their strict social laws. Because the undergrowth is so thick, they are alarmed at any unidentified rustling, and in order to prove that you are a friend (i.e. another gorilla) you have to grunt in a peaceful sort of way all the time, which reassures them. The other problem was that standing up is an aggressive posture for a gorilla: they will only stand up to thump their chests and make a threatening display. So I couldn't stand up. There I was scrambling around on these steep and thickly wooded slopes for nearly eight hours, grunting every so often and carrying a camera. I wasn't helped by the thinness of the air up there, which sapped my energy very quickly. Still, I got the pictures, and that turned out to be one of the most memorable sequences in the whole series.'

The sound recordist does not have to dance in such close attendance, but it is vital that he keeps a trained ear open for background noise. Dicky Bird is sometimes so intent on listening out for extraneous sounds that he subconsciously blocks out from his mind the actual commentary:

'Often I can listen to David chatting away and not realise that I'm concentrating on the background more than the words. David will ask me "Did I say so-and-so?", and I can only reply "Well, did you?" But the great advantage of tape over film is that I can play it back right away and check any query to make sure that no unwanted noise is creeping on to the sound track. This is particularly valuable when I have to tone down some continuous noise, such as rain or wind, which is really a matter of trial and error in the placing of the microphones. Rain doesn't present too many problems and we can always film in it provided that no drops get on the camera lens. The unfortunate side-effect of wet weather is that David has to wear a waterproof anorak, which magnifies the noise of the falling rain on the microphone into a tremendous crashing and crackling. Wind can be much more irritating, because it can spring up suddenly and die down in the same way. Often I will hold up the filming because it's blowing half a gale and when that has finally stopped the cameraman will be unable to film because the light is fading. It is a question of reaching a friendly compromise between the two of us.

'The last place you would expect trouble with man-made noise is Antarctica. Ned Kelly, Hugh Maynard and I travelled out there courtesy of the Royal Navy aboard HMS *Endurance*, and were stranded in the Falkland Islands for Christmas – but that's another story! When we eventually landed on the South Sandwich Islands I found the wind so strong that even the shields on the microphones didn't made much difference. On top of that, there was a helicopter belonging to the British Antarctic Survey team which had its own job to do, and was passing right over our heads every 30 seconds. One of the ship's officers was hunting duck nearby, and the noise of his shotgun added to my difficulties. Of course it was also very cold, and a lot of my attention was taken up with the problems of keeping warm and staying alive. We were flown off the ship in small helicopters and dropped on small islands and icebergs, so the amount of equipment we could carry was strictly limited, especially as we had to have survival packs with us at all times.

'We all had to undergo some very rigorous tests from the Navy before we were allowed to go. One of these was to have been a prac-tice jump from a helicopter into the water, but luckily the helicopter was out of action on that particular day. However, we still had to learn the techniques for surviving in an icy sea. They taught us by

Naval helicopters were both a blessing and a nuisance during the filming in the South Atlantic (*NK/BBC Enterprises*)

Ups and downs Martin Saunders trudging through mud (*AN*) to film rice planting in Malaysia (*RM*) and, later, keeping his feet clean in zero gravity (*AW*)

tossing us into a swimming pool wearing life jackets and inflatable · dinghies; we had to be able to inflate the dinghy and climb into it while it was still submerged. Once we were in and had zipped ourselves up they would roll us over again to teach us how to escape from the dinghy when we were underwater – and then climb back in again. That was something I'd never expected to come across during the making of a documentary film.'

Courage is a quality high on the list of requirements for cameramen and sound recordists. For *The Living Planet* they have climbed huge jungle trees, suspended themselves from ropes 100 feet up in the air, dodged sharks, hung out of helicopters, perched on the edge of balloon baskets, braved man-eating tigers and lived among Amazonian Indians who were known to have killed Europeans with spears. Martin Saunders, in particular, came to the series with a reputation as the BBC's 'commando cameraman', and justified it many times, especially when it came to filming big animals.

'The very first trip of the series took us to the Canadian Arctic. After some sync filming with David, the rest of the crew returned home leaving my assistant and myself to travel on to Baffin Island. Our object was to film the narwhal, a whale with a huge extended tooth which sticks out from its snout like a six-foot-long tusk. We hired a helicopter and got some shots from the air, and then asked them to dump us on an ice floe for the rest of the day. We spent three periods of eight hours each on the ice, and were lucky enough to film two narwhals fencing with their tusks, something which has never been filmed before.

'We also tried to take some shots of them underwater, but they were very timid. Diving in those waters has its unique problems. The melting ice is fresh water, which is lighter than salt water and thus stays in a layer on the top of the sea. The freezing point of fresh water is also slightly higher than that of salt water, so that as you dive down through it any fresh water caught in the nooks and crannies of your suit or equipment immediately turns into ice. The effects of this can be fatal unless you're an experienced swimmer. One day I was 50 feet down when I suddenly realised that breathing was becoming difficult and something was going very wrong with my air supply. I tapped my assistant on the shoulder, handed him the camera and at that moment the regulator on my sub-aqua equipment froze open and clouds of bubbles exploded everywhere. I shot to the surface and not much harm was done, but it was a very hairy moment. In the end I discovered that it was my fault. There is a little rubber winterising cap which you are supposed to fill with alcohol and clip on to the regulator to stop it from freezing in icy conditions: I had forgotten it. I managed to borrow a cap, but we had no alcohol. It so happened that on our journey out we had bought a bottle of the local rum called "Newfoundland Screech", so I filled the cap with some of that and it worked perfectly! When subsequently we got back to Bristol, I was unpacking the diving equipment and found the rubber cap still full of rum. We used it to drink a toast to the Arctic.

'While we were up in the North Atlantic, I was sent to film humpback whales off the coast of Maine. The whales migrate once a year to feed on the vast shoals of fish which spawn there. When a whale has located them it circles round them blowing out great bubbles which float to the surface and form a kind of corral around them. Then it dives down and comes up straight into the centre of the corral with its huge mouth open, scooping up the fish as it rises. The difficulty in filming this is that I was above the water while most of the action was going on below the surface, but on that day we hit perfect conditions. I was filming from a boat, so in order to get a high and unobstructed view I climbed out on to the bowsprit and lay there

with my camera right above the sea. It was as smooth as a mirror, and I could see the bubbles on the surface. Then the whale came up and the fish began to panic and try to get out of the way, making the water boil as this expanding shadow rose from the depths. It was an awesome sight,and because the sea was so calm I could see it all happening through the surface.'

Commando cameraman Martin Saunders about to dive in pursuit of whales in the Arctic (*AW*)

Next to courage comes adaptability. Interspersed with the moments of high drama and danger can be long periods of patient immobility, when the cameraman has to sit silent and still in a hide waiting for perhaps a few seconds of action. The phlegmatic Hugh Maynard is as accustomed as anyone can be to such vicissitudes; but, even by his standards, the two-month trip to South America at the beginning of 1982 was a complicated, constantly surprising and sometimes hair-raising one. A condensed narrative graphically demonstrates the variety of calls that were made upon his skills.

The journey began in January, when Hugh and Adrian Warren flew to Paramaribo, the capital of Surinam on the north-east coast of South America. Their aim was to film the group courtship display of the cock-of-the-rock bird, a dazzling orange forest-dweller. Having been joined by a local ornithologist who knew where the birds were to be found, they hired a boat and set off upriver into the interior. A camp was set up in the forest, about half-an-hour's tramp from the location. After a good, honest, English breakfast of porridge ('a pretty silly way to start', Hugh thought) they would walk to the hide and be in position well before dawn each day, so as to be ready before the birds began their daily business. The gloom under the forest canopy made them hard to film unless they moved into a patch of sunlight.

Sitting still for several hours at a stretch demands a lot of patience, especially in the sweltering humidity of a jungle where the temperature rose to $75\,°F$ an hour after sunrise. Hugh's problems were compounded by a mysterious itching which started at his ankles and gradually made its way up his legs. Very soon his legs were completely covered in bites, all inflicted by the tiny grass lice which swarmed beneath his feet. The ornithologist, however, was unaffected. He had brought a special spray to keep the creatures off his own feet, but for some reason best known to himself had not warned his companion.

After a long and cramped day in the hide, they all looked forward to the time when they could clamber into their hammocks and get some sleep. Adrian set his alarm clock every night to make sure that they woke early enough. However, they had reckoned without the talents of a local frog, whose night call was a faithful copy of the

The cock-of-the-rock Filmed in Surinam with enormous patience by Hugh Maynard (*AW/BBC Enterprises*)

alarm. 'It would go off at about 3 o'clock in the morning', Hugh remembers. 'I'd swing out of my hammock and collapse on to the ground half-asleep, grab my clothes and then realise, to my horror, what the real time was. It was the perfect mimic of our clock.' The team grew surprisingly fond of this beast, and affectionately christened it the 'Seiko Frog'.

That was just the first of 21 locations which had been planned for the trip. From Surinam, Hugh and Adrian flew on to Quito in Ecuador, high up in the Andes, where they joined Richard Brock. Tony Morrison, author of the Time–Life book on the Andes, fluent Spanish speaker and past master at dealing with South American red tape, had also been persuaded to join the party. He swept the newcomers through customs and immigration control in record time, but then a major snag came to light – they had run out of film! Hugh had used up his supply of stock in Surinam, and a new batch was supposed to have arrived in Quito from Bristol. It had simply vanished and none of the right type (Eastmancolour 7247) was available in Ecuador. The crisis was a considerable one. A film crew is an expensive thing to run: a team of five people on the road costs more than £600 a day in salaries, expenses and other outgoings, so a producer cannot afford to leave it idle. Quite apart from the waste and frustration that a delay causes, there was a tight schedule to be kept to which had been planned by Beth Huntley with great care in

Bristol six months before. The only solution was for Adrian Warren, only a few hours after his arrival, to catch another plane up to Miami, there to pick up the precious film and fly straight back to Quito through the night.

Three days later, the party was heading through dense cloud in an unpressurised DC3 belonging to an American group with a base in the Amazon jungle. As they flew over the Andes sucking oxygen from plastic tubes, Richard Brock couldn't help recalling the famous 'Alive!' aircraft disaster of 1972, in which the survivors of a plane crash in the mountains had been forced to feed off those who had been killed. It was a relief to land on the grass airstrip at Limoncocha, where they were greeted by Jim Yost, an anthropologist working at the American camp.

The veteran DC-3 which took the crew over the Andes – just! (*RB*)

The main purpose of the trip was to film the local Waorani Indians for the programme 'Jungle', in order to demonstrate how man could still live in close harmony with his natural environment. The Waorani had a fearsome reputation. For centuries they had lived undisturbed in the Amazon jungle, and did not always take kindly to intruders. They used blowpipes and poison darts for hunting their food, and in the past had been known to turn against white men who disturbed their privacy. In the 1960s they had killed four missionaries, and more recently were reported to have disposed of two oil prospectors. Luckily, Jim Yost knew the tribesmen better than any other outsider. He had spent nine years getting to know them and their language and customs, and had succeeded in gaining their trust. The progress of the filming – perhaps even the safety of the cameraman – depended to a large extent on his guidance and influence.

Yost, accompanied by Hugh Maynard, boarded a Cessna aircraft and flew to an airstrip on the banks of the Cononaco River. The strip was so tiny that Hugh Maynard couldn't see it from the air, even when the pilot pointed it out to him! They were met by a party of Indians who were to guide them to the Waorani camp. First, however, they had to cross the river: there were no bridges, and it was the flood season. Fortunately, this problem had been foreseen by the research team six months earlier and, faithful to the instructions on the schedule, they had bought two inflatable dinghies in Miami especially for the crossing. These were meant for ferrying the camera gear rather than the men, so Hugh had to strip off and swim the river, pushing one dinghy in front of him. The swirling water was muddy and flowing fast, and here and there a jagged tree-branch poked above the surface. The current pushed Hugh over 200 yards downstream before he reached the opposite bank, but he was reassured by the knowledge that there would be no piranha in such a spate.

Friends in the forest Adrian
Warren and the Waorani, deep
in the forests of Ecuador (*AW*)

Any personal trepidation he might have felt evaporated as soon as
he met the welcoming party of Waorani. They were open-hearted
and affectionate, and when they realised that the cameraman posed
no sort of threat they were all smiles. The smiles broadened when Jim
Yost introduced him as 'Hugh': in their language, the sound 'hew'
apparently means 'spit'. They began the trek through the jungle
to the Indian camp, an utterly exhausting experience for the
Englishman:

'They were all superbly built – about five feet high and five feet wide
and muscular with it. This was just as well because they had to carry
all my equipment. Jim had told me not to bother carrying anything,
but I thought I ought to show willing and set off with my small
tripod. After a couple of hours I had to hand it to one of the Indians:
it was all I could do to walk, or rather run, because that's how fast
I had to go to keep up with them. The paths through the forest were
wet and slippery, and so difficult to make out that if I had lagged
behind I'd have been lost. As it was I floundered about and often had

to be helped up the slopes by a crowd of children who were running about and laughing their heads off.

'Their camp consisted of a big communal mud hut made of wooden stakes and woven leaves in which they all lived, ate and slept. We were given hammocks to sleep in, but as the Indians are five feet tall and I am six feet tall I wasn't too comfortable at nights. They are a very affable people, and a lot of our time was spent sitting around in hammocks – often as many as six to one hammock, and all stark naked – and chattering. I enjoy being with "primitive" peoples, because they are almost completely relaxed in their surroundings and suffer none of the stresses that we so-called "civilised" people are prone to. As gifts we took them some mirrors, but all they really wanted were combs. They had lovely black hair (although it was full of lice) and were delighted when I gave them my solitary comb.

'The one thing I didn't enjoy was the food. When we arrived, they had just polished off the last of the dried monkey for that season, so the staple diet consisted almost entirely of a kind of palm nut. They gather great mounds of these nuts, boil them up for a few hours adding water occasionally, and turn it into a soggy mess. Throughout the nut season they just drink water and eat this mush. I hadn't brought any food of my own so I had no choice but to eat with them – and I didn't enjoy the experience. It had a strange taste, less appetising than other nuts and much softer, and sometimes it started fermenting in the heat. The Waorani thrived on it, and developed big guts during the nut season, but they all stayed very fit.'

Hugh Maynard gets a close shot of a Waorani hunting with his blowpipe (*AW*)

While Hugh began his filming of the Waorani, Richard Brock and Adrian Warren set off from Limoncocha by dug-out canoe to a jungle lodge called Primavera. This had originally been built to house a hoped-for flood of tourists, who were expected to travel to this remote spot to see the jungle. The owner of Primavera had even gone to the lengths of building a system of scaffolding and ladders round the trunk of one of the giant kapok trees so that his guests could stand on the very roof of the rainforest. The tree made a perfect setting for David Attenborough to illustrate the different layers of life in a jungle. Once all the equipment had been stowed at Primavera, Richard Brock travelled back to Limoncocha to meet Attenborough, Dicky Bird and assistant cameraman Jerry Gould, who were arriving by plane from Miami. They stayed the night in a modest hotel rejoicing in the grand name of the Hotel Amazonas, where they ate an execrable catfish risotto. Hugh Maynard's stomach wasn't the only one to suffer!

No stars   The crew check into the grandly-named Hotel Amazonas (*RB*)

Hugh rejoined the party in mid-February with a rucksackful of unique footage of the Waorani, including a sequence on the preparation of their deadly poison darts. The next task was a sync filming of David Attenborough perched amid the vegetation that grew on the massive limbs of the kapok tree. It was a bewitching experience for up there above the forest canopy was a self-contained world of flowering bromeliads and communities of birds, lizards, frogs and insects. Meanwhile, in another part of the jungle, Adrian Warren had expended an enormous amount of energy and ingenuity in the fixing of an arrangement of ropes by which David Attenborough could be filmed actually climbing a tree. He was given an instant course in rope climbing and spoke his piece to the camera at varying heights and degrees of discomfort.

The last job in Ecuador took them south once again to the beautiful gorge in the Andes at Baños. Luck plays a large part in the success of an intricately-planned expedition such as this, and now the crew enjoyed two strokes of it. The first was the filming of the snow-capped peaks of the extinct volcano, which was needed for the 'Frozen world' programme and had to be done en route to an entirely different location. With vast clouds wreathing the mountain as they approached, there seemed to be little hope of a satisfactory shot. Suddenly, however, the clouds lifted just long enough for Hugh Maynard to get the view he needed and then just as suddenly closed in again. The second piece of luck came at Baños. The crew was threading its way down a rough road in the Paztaza gorge, and far below the chocolate-coloured river (a tributary of the Amazon) was plunging to the forest plain. Richard Brock was searching for a water-fall which would show the force with which the young river cuts through the rock. By chance, they eventually found the perfect spot – not just a stretch of fast-moving water, but beside it an empty flood channel. This gave a graphic illustration of the way in which the sand in the current had polished the river's rocky sides, and how great boulders had been shifted by the power of the water. It was a bonus that would add greatly to the impact of this particular sequence.

Even with all this good fortune, they were only just keeping up with the schedule. An incredible amount of work had been packed into a mere 11 days in Ecuador, yet still there was no margin for relaxation. Hired trucks had to be returned, detailed lists of equipment (in both English and Spanish) had to be stamped by the proper authority, hotel bookings had to be confirmed, cans of exposed film had to be shipped back to England, receptions had to be attended, and helpers had to be paid and thanked. Finally, there was a plane to catch for Lima, in Peru, where a varied, not to say enigmatic, 'shopping list' of items to be filmed had been drawn up:

Rope trick Setting up the ropes ready for David Attenborough to climb a giant kapok tree (*David Attenborough*)

- source of Amazon from glacier
- torrent ducks (and surrounding vegetation?)
- David and vicuna at La Raya
- condors at Paracas
- bottles in bay at Paracas
- Guano Islands
- try to pick something up at source or Manaus to show at Belem as having floated down Amazon!

Map labels (within figure):

Miami, USA — Aruba — Curaçao — Caracas — Miami, USA — 6 Feb. Trinidad — AW + HM — AW 21 Feb. — HM — AW + HM ex UK 22 Jan. — AW 23 Feb.

VENEZUELA — Georgetown — AW 21 Feb. — Paramaribo — cock of the rock birds — SURINAM — FRENCH GUIANA — GUYANA

COLOMBIA — 6 Feb. — RB + DA/JG + DB — 10 Feb. — 19 Feb. — AW HM — 8 Feb. — all 4 March — RM 3 March

Equator — Quito — Waorani Indians — DA up tree — rivers — Lotopaxi volcano — ECUADOR — Guayaquil

Manaus — all 6 March — DA and giant waterlily — Belém — Mouth of the Amazon and DA

PERU — all 1 March — BRAZIL — all 14 March — all 10 March

all 20 Feb. — RB 13 March

Lima — all 21 Feb. — Cuzco 22 Feb. — Sicuani — source of the Amazon — torrent ducks — all 24 Feb. — Paracas — DA on guano islands — BOLIVIA — Brasília — DA on grasslands and giant anteater — 6 March RM — 12 March RB

CHILE — PARAGUAY — RB + HM 11 March — Rio de Janiero

Tropic of Capricorn — ARGENTINA — URUGUAY — Iguassu Falls

Transverse Mercator Projection — © Oxford University

Key
AW   Adrian Warren, director
HM   Hugh Maynard, cameraman
RB   Richard Brock, producer
DB   Dickie Bird, sound recordist
JG   Jerry Gould, assistant cameraman
RM   Richard Matthews, assistant produce
DA   David Attenborough, presenter

All locations were also visited by Tony Morris a few days prior to the rest of the crew, to confirm filming plans

There are several places that claim to be the source of the Amazon, as John Waters had already discovered, but Richard Brock had decided on Sicuani, high in the mountains near Cuzco, an area he described as 'not unlike the Brecon Beacons'. Breathing was likely to become a problem at such a height, so as a precaution the crew planned to collect a cylinder of oxygen before pressing on. But it was a Sunday and anywhere in Cuzco that might have supplied oxygen cylinders was most definitely closed. They loaded their equipment into a hired truck and station wagon and headed for Sicuani through thick mud and driving rain. Luck was still with them, however, taking the form of a diversion caused by a collapsed bridge. They passed through a village where the locals had built a flimsy looking structure across the river – and were charging a small toll for the dubious privilege of using it. Then suddenly, rounding a bend, they spotted a distant speck on a boulder – appropriately and most welcome, a torrent duck. These ducks were known to be in the vicinity, but to find one so close at hand was a godsend. By now the rain had almost stopped, and Hugh Maynard and Jerry Gould quickly set up the camera. The torrent duck began preening itself on the rock in its own charming way, taking next to no notice of the cameramen as they gradually crept forward. It had obviously read the script, because it intermittently dived and swam in the torrent exactly as they had hoped.

Torrent duck in Peru (*Gunter Ziesler/Bruce Coleman Ltd*)

However carefully the producer and his team plan a schedule, in the end it can be the small unpredictable occurrences that trip them up. This was nearly the case with the source of the Amazon filming and the oxygen, for after the happy accident of the torrent duck, an incident occurred which almost ended in tragedy. Richard Brock had managed to borrow some oxygen cylinders from the Sicuani hospital, and next day the party started for the snowline, about 12 000 feet up. They were looking for a location with wetness much in evidence, suitable for illustrating the birth of a great river. Conditions were miserable, and the rattling of hailstones made it impossible for Dicky Bird to record anything. As they waited for the hail to turn to rain, Hugh saw that his assistant was in trouble: 'We looked at Jerry and he'd gone a dark shade of blue. It must have been a combination of lack of oxygen and the cold. We bundled him into the car, warmed him up and gave him a whiff of oxygen; he soon cheered up again.'

By now, not surprisingly, the party was beginning to show signs of wear and tear. Hugh, especially, was suffering from a pain in his guts which he put down to poor food and incessant rain. In fact he had worms, which he had caught from the monotonous and tasteless nut mush of the Waorani, although he was not to know this until he returned to England. Morale was not helped, either, by the temp-

(Above) A condor in Peru,
(below) sealions (*Keith Scholey*)

orary disappearance of the equipment on the way to Lima. But the filming continued to go well. The wild and spectacular coastline near Paracas is an important wildlife preserve, and yielded useful footage of sea lions and turkey vultures, though none of the Andean condors specified on the 'shopping list'.

The crew also filmed on the famous Guano Islands, where a once lucrative trade in manure has been destroyed by man's over-fishing. The seabird whose generous droppings contained a large proportion of half-digested anchovy – a valuable source of agricultural fertiliser – had disappeared from the islands when its food source ran out. This man-made gap in the food chain made a forceful case study for the final programme in the series, 'New worlds'. Although the script for that programme (to be produced by Andrew Neal) was still in outline form, Richard Brock felt that this dramatic example of the collapse of a wild population and its consequences was worth filming because they had the opportunity, the time and the crew available. 'If you have the chance, film it' is one of the golden rules of documentary production.

For the last item on the Peruvian leg of their journey, the crew had to stumble about between the recumbent bodies of an all too numerous species – *Homo sapiens*. Richard and Hugh were trying to get pictures of the friendly little sanderlings, birds which move like massed clockwork toys along the shore of Paracas beach. Unfortunately it was a Sunday, and the beach was intermittently invaded by crowds of sun-bathing Peruvians disembarking from tourist boats. Hugh set up a remote-controlled camera and camouflaged it with brushwood and seaweed. As it transpired, he had disguised it so well that passers-by kept blundering into it and kicking it over. The birds were so disturbed by the human activity that they retreated to the far end of the beach, and Richard Brock had to make several forlorn attempts to drive them back within camera range. After trotting over miles of sand he and Hugh were forced to admit defeat. *Homo sapiens* had struck again, as he was to do during the next piece of filming, 1300 miles away in Manaus, Brazil.

Having already filmed the source of the Amazon, the crew's next job was to cover the 'middle age' of the river. For specific local knowledge, Richard Brock had turned to a swarthy Brazilian ichthyologist, who agreed to help just so long as he was rewarded with a large amount of caviare. It turned out that this had been the price fixed by a previous television crew (not a BBC one, of course) and so an expensive precedent had been set. Richard hastily looked elsewhere and found an excellent substitute whose crafty way with officialdom soon earned him the nickname of 'Señor Fixit'.

They boarded an eccentric-looking two-storey motorboat and set

off across the river in search of the giant waterlily. One would have thought that a patch of the largest leaves in the world would be easy to find, but it was only after a great deal of toing and froing that a distant patch of them was spotted. David Attenborough transferred into a minute dug-out canoe borrowed from a local fisherman and paddled into a suitable position, ready to speak his piece to the camera. Hugh Maynard, on the upstairs balcony of the boat, had an elevated vantage point which gave a good idea of the scale of the waterlilies. However, it soon became apparent that they had picked on a local beauty spot. Dicky Bird had impossible problems with his sound recording, what with children shouting, boats chugging by, aircraft buzzing overhead, transistor radios blaring and even a distant chain-saw whining. Whenever there was a brief interval of silence, a cloud would hurriedly arrive to blot out the sun. On top of all this, the local botanical adviser began demanding more money, because he felt that his skills as an interpreter were being over-used in shouting at the tripper boats. But somehow the sequence was shot to everyone's satisfaction and sanity was restored. Indeed, they were now ahead of schedule – a rare luxury.

David Attenborough waits patiently among the waterlilies for the noise to stop and the sun to come out (*RB*)

The final location was the spectacular *Falls of Iguassu*, where the Parana descends through the jungle in a series of splendid cascades. In order to film the river's effect on the rock structure, *Hugh* and *Richard* had to get airborne, and so they arranged to hire a *helicopter* from a local firm. 'It was without doubt the smallest helicopter I have been in', Hugh remembers ruefully. 'We thought it was a one-man aircraft, although it had two seats. In fact three of us had to cram ourselves into it, which meant that I was hanging virtually on the outside of my camera. The wind was gusting and threw us about, but it was thrilling rather than frightening.'

At last this extraordinary trip was over. In six weeks, the party had travelled nearly 30 000 miles; they had filmed deep in the tropical rainforest, high in the *Andes*, and down on the Pacific shore; they had stayed in a no-star 'Hotel *Amazanos*' in the jungle with almost no furniture and in a four-star 'Hotel Amazonas' in *Manaus* with air-conditioning and colour television; they had seen the *Waorani* Indians living in harmony with nature, and the effect of man's abuse of nature. And, for Hugh Maynard at least, the journey had a gently ironic ending. When the team finally dispersed at *Rio de Janeiro*, most people flew back to England, but Hugh and *Jerry Gould* travelled north to *Miami* to meet their wives and take a well-earned rest. It just so happened that they arrived in Miami as the very first NASA Space Shuttle was about to be launched. Although Hugh was off duty, he could not resist the opportunity, and at 3 o'clock the next morning he was on the beach along with hundreds of other sightseers – setting up his own camera for yet another shot.

The magnificent Falls of Iguassu A fitting climax to an exciting and complex trip (*RM/BBC Enterprises*)

THE LONERS
Two freelance film-makers

The wildlife film-maker is in many ways the modern equivalent of the big game hunter. He shoots film instead of bullets, but has to call on many of the same qualities – great physical toughness, an instinctive understanding of how animals think and above all monumental patience. He also needs technical skill, agility, determination in the face of obstacles both human and natural, the ability to improvise and a phlegmatic attitude towards possible failure. It is hardly surprising that most of them prefer to work alone.

There are bound to be a few failures, even on the best-organised shooting trips, but a cameraman has to be judged by whether or not he can bring back the goods. The freelance specialists who were hired to film sequences for *The Living Planet* were people who could be relied on to find the right species doing the right things, and get that on celluloid by the right date. Within this simple formula, constricted by the demands of the budget, some astonishing footage was obtained of many rare or elusive creatures. In this chapter two award-winning film-makers described some of the particular problems and rewards of working on the series.

Top of the tree Neil Rettig
perched in the forest canopy
(*AW*)

Neil Rettig

One of the most frustrating experiences of my whole life occurred while I was filming for this series. Adrian Warren had sent my brother and myself to Malaysia to film – or try to film – the Sumatran rhino. This had never been done before; in fact hardly anyone had ever seen the animal, as it was extremely shy and extremely rare, with only about 150 individuals left in the wild. We were told by the researchers that it was very afraid of any human disturbance, and that the only likely location for finding a specimen was at one of the mud 'wallows' where they like to bathe occasionally.

The rhino is so sensitive that if a human so much as walks near one of the wallows it will abandon the whole area for days, weeks and even months. They have well-developed senses of smell and hearing, but luckily for us their eyesight is very poor. So, in order to keep our scent from ground level, we built platforms about 20 feet up in the jungle trees, 60 feet or so from one of these wallows, so that we had a fairly clear camera angle. We had red amber lights rigged up and powered by 12-volt batteries to provide some extra ambient lighting when we used night vision lenses in the dark. On top of the platform we built a hide – what we Americans call a 'blind' – so that we could watch without being seen.

There was another cameraman with us, and he did the first spell in the blind, watching and waiting for this elusive creature. After two days and two nights I took over from him. He hadn't seen a whisker of a rhino, and I thought, 'They haven't appeared for him, so they're bound to appear for me!' I was going to be stuck up there for quite a while, so I asked my brother to go off and fetch some provisions. The only difficulty was: when was the best time for him to return so that he didn't disturb the wildlife? We decided that the best time for this would be mid-day, when the sun is at its hottest and few animals are stirring.

So off he went to get the food, and I settled down to wait. Living in a blind 20 feet up in a rainforest is not really a lot of fun. You have to sit still and concentrate on watching for the animals to come. That forest was the hottest I have ever been in because the leaf canopy, which normally shelters the ground from the direct sunlight, was broken in several places. The sun just poured through, and by mid-morning it was sweltering. The humidity was so great that there was water everywhere, and no matter how tightly we sealed the roof, the tropical rains would filter through. I tried to sleep at nights with the water dripping on to my face and soaking my sleeping bag. It was like an ancient Chinese torture. Even the normal day-to-day activities become a lot more complicated. One of the hardest things to solve is what to do with your waste. You can urinate into a big plastic container, but what happens when that's full? You have to carry it a long way away so that the scent won't disturb the rhino, but if you start climbing down from the blind you may disturb it anyway: you just have to live with it, no matter how grubby and messy everything becomes.

I sat and watched all during that morning but nothing happened, and deep down I was beginning to feel that nothing ever would happen. Then, at about 11.30, I heard a noise coming through the forest. There were ponderous footsteps, rustling and a muffled grunting getting closer and closer. After all the planning and waiting I could barely believe it. It kept coming closer and I focused the camera on the spot where I thought it would emerge and started to squeeze the shutter release. Then I heard a noise over on the right which sounded like another one coming so I carefully peered out. There was my brother holding a bag of lunch, staring at me as pale as a ghost. The rhino saw him and took off into the jungle and that was that. I just sat there in the blind trembling and feeling really sick.

By a weird coincidence, my brother was the only person who actually came face to face with a rhino on that trip. He's probably one of the very few people to have seen one at all in recent years. We were keeping a close watch on two wallows, and one of them had

Neil and his brother Joel Rettig (left) share most of their filming and recording work (*AW*)

barely any signs of rhino activity at all, no tracks or droppings. I asked my brother to go and check out that wallow to see if there were any new tracks there. As he approached he looked down, not expecting to see anything special, but there, about eight feet away from him, was a Sumatran rhino. It jumped up, ran a few yards, stopped and stared: few humans had ever been so close. My brother backed up and ran all the way back to the blind to fetch me, but of course by the time I got there it had disappeared. To this day – as far as I know – the species still hasn't been filmed.

I call it a frustrating experience, but in fact we would have been very lucky to have got film of such a rare animal. We had the chance but not the luck. You can't spend too much time waiting for a single animal to appear, because that uses up a lot of money. We had trained the camera on one particular spot, so we couldn't film anything else, even though there were plenty of other interesting things going on all around us. The rhino was to be an exciting part of the programme, and therefore it was worth restricting all our efforts to that. We didn't succeed, but we certainly tried!

In a tree by a wallow Waiting for the rhinos (*AW*)

Animals which are shy of man are obviously going to be difficult to film, but even inanimate objects like plants sometimes cause us headaches. One of our other assignments in Malaysia was to try and film the phenomenon called 'big bang flowering', which occurs in the rainforests there every once in a while. Masses of trees flower at the same time, and the forest can look like a carpet of colour with every shade imaginable. It's an entirely unpredictable event, somehow tied in with the dry season, and may happen only once every six years. When I was there it didn't happen but we were able to find isolated patches of flowering trees, from which we could give the impression that there was an ocean of flowers all around. We found a tree, climbed 160 feet to the top, built a platform and spent an hour or two filming. That's the first time I've ever built a platform just for one brief shot and never gone back to it again.

I use blinds in a lot of my filming., but they are not always stuck up at the top of forest trees. Sometimes, they're not even fixed to anything at all. When I was in Argentina, Richard Matthews asked me to shoot some footage of the rhea, a flightless bird rather like the ostrich which lives out on the pampas there. We needed film of the chicks hatching from the eggs, which are laid in nests on the ground. One major snag was that the adult birds get very touchy about their nest sites and will abandon the eggs if they are disturbed too often. The other was that we arrived on location a little too late in the season – my schedule was so crowded that I couldn't get down there any sooner. My assistant had gone ahead, but he was finding that all the eggs seemed to be hatched, and of course as soon as that happens, the whole family moves off. The first few attempts at shooting were hopeless – as soon as I approached with my camera on my shoulder the birds galloped away into the distance.

Neil Rettig makes friends with a rhea chick (*NR*)

We were desperate to figure out a way of getting closer to them. Then came the moment of inspiration – we would make a dummy rhea! I could stand inside it with my camera peeking out of the front and fool them into thinking I was a bird. It may sound crazy but we couldn't dream up any other workable ideas. So I rang up Richard Matthews and told him; he warned me that the rheas become very aggressive when they're with their young and could very well attack me. This was not exactly cheering news, but all the same we got down to making the dummy. The framework was wire netting, and over the top of that was papier mâché painted the right colour. It took a day and a half to finish, and then I took it out onto the pampas, crawled inside and set off towards the birds. They took one look and ran away faster and farther than ever before!

That is about the most comical situation I've been in while shooting, and it just goes to show that you shouldn't be afraid to

Rhea view This dummy took a day and a half to make, but it didn't fool the birds, who took one look and left their nests (*NR*)

experiment. We had come up with several other ideas which were just as nutty, such as building a blind to look like a dead cow, but in the end at least the dummy rhea allowed me to get a little bit of film. Later we were lucky enough to find a nest with eggs that were still being incubated, and were able to use the more traditional method of the moveable blind. This involves building a blind that blends in with the landscape and gradually moving it closer and closer to the birds, maybe over a period of days. They become used to the blind, and, because they can't see any humans in it, they don't get scared.

Things aren't always as easy as that, however, especially when you're at the mercy of the weather. For instance, filming for this series seems to have got me caught up in a number of floods. We were in a national park in Malaysia when the rains came and cut us off: we had to string cables across the river and haul our camera equipment over on pulleys because the only bridge had been washed away.

Later, Andrew Neal asked me to shoot some film of a flash flood for the programme on deserts. It doesn't rain very often in the desert, but when it does it rains hard, and the water simply flows off the top of the bone dry soil without soaking in. The power of the water carves deep channels in the surface. These are dry gullies most of the time, but a flash flood can strike so suddenly that a wall of water can be tearing down them in a matter of minutes. I made a couple of reconnaissance trips to the Arizona desert and found the perfect spot for filming right on the bank of a dry channel. I set up a small canopy there to shelter the camera from the wet – although at that moment the weather was so hot that rain seemed impossible. After that, as in all my work, it was just a matter of sitting and waiting.

When the storm eventually began I was away over on the other side of Tucson, so I had to jump in the car and drive out to the spot as fast as I could with the rain right behind me and the wind blowing at about 50 miles an hour. I reached the shelter but I couldn't see a thing through the hail. The storm was howling all around and it suddenly dawned on me that if I didn't get out of there fast I might be swept away: they say that as many people are killed by floods in the desert as die from the heat. I ran back to the car through a barrage of hailstones that were the size of pebbles, and saw that the water in the gully was already 15 feet high. It was roaring down and undermining the road where I had parked, and the telephone wires were whipping about like crazy as if they were about to crash down on me at any moment. I was trapped because the road in front of me and behind me had been washed away. The only thing I could do was grab the camera when it stopped raining and film the desert as it turned into an ocean before me. It was an unbelievable sight, with a great torrent of brown water carrying cactus and other plants over what had once been parched earth. There are road signs out there which say 'Do Not Enter When Flooded', and when you pass them in the summer with a blue sky overhead you can't imagine where a flood can come from. It was five hours before bulldozers and other machinery arrived from Tucson to rebuild the road. Strangely enough, that was the first flash flood there had been in the area for ten years, so I was lucky to catch it on film. I suppose I was lucky not to be drowned as well!

Filming in zoos is quite a challenge, because you have to keep cages and other man-made objects out of camera shot. There are also people to contend with. At one stage I was working inside a hot house which enclosed a tropical rainforest exhibit; it was a weekend and I guess more than 3000 people must have walked through on the day I was there. I had my lighting gear set up right across one of the walkways and the electrical cable fixed down with tape. People

Adrian Warren with some of the huge hailstones which fell in Texas (*AW*)

wandered about looking up at the exhibit and invariably bumping into my tripod, kicking the cable, or knocking the lights over. Then of course they all asked me what I was doing, and I got hoarse explaining about the series, about David Attenborough, about the BBC and so on.

Equipment is my biggest headache. Even if I keep it down to a minimum for air travel there's still plenty to carry, both in bulk and in weight. On a trip to Malaysia recently I was charged US$3000 just for excess baggage. It is daunting to arrive at a big airport milling with crowds and to try and wade through them all clutching heavy cases and tripods. You have to stagger to a taxi, hope your hotel booking is all right, and find a safe place to store all your gear. Out on location it can be even worse because you are carrying every item of equipment on your own body. When I was in Costa Rica with Adrian Warren we had a half-hour walk every day from the house to

Neil Rettig tackles jungle filming in (left to right) Papua New Guinea, Costa Rica and Peru, and (above) juggles with a piranha in Venezuela (*AW/NR*)

the filming location, each of us carrying over 130 lb because we had to take ropes and climbing tackle as well as the camera equipment. First I loaded up Adrian by sticking one backpack on his shoulders and another on his chest, then I did the same for myself. Everyone was in hysterics because they could only see the bottoms of our legs poking out beneath the packs. By the end of a long day's shooting we felt pretty weak.

I worry about how the equipment is going to perform – whether cameras are going to break down, whether lenses are going to get scratched and so on – but most of all I worry about the film stock itself. When a project is finished, you have all these little bags of film which are too bulky to carry on to the plane so they have to go with the rest of the cargo. Throughout the flight you're thinking of all the terrible things that could happen to it: is some baggage handler going to leave it out on the runway in the blazing sun where it may heat up to 150 °F and turn red? You can only shoot things once, and at the heart of the job are those little cans which contain all the money and energy and hoping and planning that has gone into it.

Wildlife filming involves a lot of very hard work, and if you stuck to a nine-to-five routine you'd probably miss the best hours of the day for lighting or behaviour. Out in the field you're working 12 or maybe 15 hours a day, and when you arrive back at base and dump your camera cases that's not the end of it. You've got to clean your equipment, unload film, package it, reload the cameras, fill out reports, make notes and, if there's no one else to cook, you've got to make yourself a meal. Sometimes we've even gone out to shoot at night. When we were in Venezuela we worked from dawn to sunset, went back and had something to eat and then walked out to the

swamps again and filmed frogs for five hours. It's tough, but when you see the results, it's worth it.

A lot of people are envious of a job like mine. They don't realise that travelling all over the world and living such a hectic lifestyle can age a person pretty quickly! Being a freelancer I don't have an office to go to when I'm not in the field. If I'm not in the field then I'm not working, and if I'm not working then I'm not making any money: but when I am working, I'm never at home. I could say that a good year is when I'm away filming all the time, but that's also a bad year because I'm not home. Cameraman tend to have a high divorce rate.

On the other hand we often have a good time on location. When my brother and I were out in Venezuela with Adrian Warren we were camping at a site which was also used by a local university. We trudged wearily back one evening and there were a dozen bikini-clad co-eds taking showers from a hosepipe: I thought it was a mirage. To cut a long story short, we had a wild party that night with plenty of beer, and watched the sun come up. Next morning Adrian (who was feeling just as bad as I was) said 'Neil, I want you to go and film jaguars today.' The nearby zoo had a big enclosure with two jaguars in it, so we put a board across one corner on top of the wire fencing about 12 feet up. There was just enough room for me to sit on a little stool with my camera and tripod. It was a hot day and before long I fell asleep. I must have been out for over an hour before I was woken by the scientific adviser hissing at me. If I'd fallen in the enclosure the cats would probably have gone for me because all the visitors made them jumpy. That was a scary moment, but after all the party had been a lot of fun!

A long shot Hugh Miles filming polar bears in Radstock Bay, Canada (*NK*)

Hugh Miles

The main problem with polar bears or tigers is that they might actually eat you. Wildlife filming is not normally a dangerous activity: the cameraman's objective is to get as close as he can to an animal without disturbing its natural behaviour so that he can obtain the best possible shots. In the vast majority of cases he will be perfectly safe provided he doesn't do anything stupid. There are very few animals which will attack a human for no good reason, but bears and tigers are among them, and I have been closely involved with both during the making of this series.

In the summer of 1981 I went up into the Arctic Circle in the far north of Canada with Ned Kelly to try and film polar bears. We particularly wanted footage of them hunting ringed seals, something which has never been filmed successfully before. Our base was a hut belonging to the scientist Ian Stirling, which was perched on a rock about 600 feet above sea level. This was a reasonably safe spot because the climb up was difficult enough to discourage any inquisitive bears, and we felt that we could sleep easily. It was the brief period of the Arctic summer with 24 hours of daylight, so we were able to keep a watch round the clock. We could see for huge distances across the ice where the polar bears would prowl waiting for ringed

seals to pop up for air. As soon as a bear was spotted we would slither down from our vantage point and rush to another smaller rock from where we did the shooting. This one was 20 feet high and we thought we were safe enough until Ian told us that he had once seen a polar bear climb 20 feet in one bound!

Once we were stationed behind the camera we would wait and hope that the bear would come closer. The ice is flat so you can always see them, but there is always the risk that they will attack you. They are really inquisitive rather than aggressive, especially the pre-adult ones, and they are usually hungry. If a young one kills a seal, for instance, an adult will often bully it off its prey and eat the seal itself. The result is that there is some hungry and disgruntled bears about and if they smell you they will certainly come to investigate and perhaps stalk you as well. There are many stories of Arctic travellers being hunted by polar bears. As they can grow to eight feet tall and weigh over 900 lb, you wouldn't stand much chance unarmed, so one of us always carried a rifle. If the bear attacks you simply have to shoot it, and if the gun jams in the cold then you're a goner. A scientist we knew had a gun jam on him one day, but luckily he was carrying a Colt 45 as well: by the time he shot the bear it was so close that it fell at his feet. And that's a waste of a perfectly good bear which was only behaving naturally – none of us wants a bear killed.

A bear hunts seal on the vast flatness of the Arctic ice – it may seem a good way off, but it can close the gap rapidly with a shambling gallop (*NK*)

Bear-watching with protection against the glare of the snow (*NK*)

Ian Stirling's hut (*HM*)

We had to use the gun on a couple of occasions, but only to frighten the animals away by firing over their heads. The first was when a female came to feed on a dead seal which was fairly near our little rock. There was another female close by with cubs which we would rather have filmed so we tried to scare the first one off by waving our arms and throwing stones on to the ice. This was a wrong move, because she promptly started coming towards us and circling round to get our scent. She was looking particularly aggressive with her head down and her ears back. Ned put a bullet over her head and she didn't bat an eyelid so we knew we were in trouble – it was either her or us. Luckily another bear came running towards the seal just then, and she decided to defend her meal rather than attack us. By that time she was only 20 yards away, but I had been filming steadily all the while and had got a very good close-up shot of her face. On the other occasion we were packing up and had all our gear stacked on the edge of the ice waiting for the helicopter to pick us up. A young bear became interested, and we had to retreat away from the equipment and back up the rock. My assistant had to fire four times before the bear went off.

After I had been out there for three weeks I began to feel much more confident. The experience of being close to these great predators makes you familiar with the way they behave and you can quickly sense danger – which in fact makes you less scared. The important lesson with all animals is learning how to read their moods and judge how they are feeling. You can soon tell whether they are inquisitive or scared or starting to become aggressive. To back this up, I had made a point of reading everything I could find on polar bears before I left England, including the latest research papers. One of the basic rules of my job is to know what an animal will do in certain circumstances so that you can anticipate it and photograph it properly.

In spite of the ever-present danger, I felt it was a privilege to be in such a beautiful place. It was so remote that I could never have afforded to go there at my own expense; I had to keep pinching myself to make sure that I was actually being paid for staying there. The sun shone across the bay most of the time, glistening on the huge band of ice and causing a heat haze that made it difficult for me to use my long-distance lenses. Towards the end of July the ice broke up and half of it drifted away on the tides. This resulted in massive turbulence in the bay and huge numbers of seabirds flew in to feed on the fish which were churned up. There were harp seals and white whales swimming round just below us – I didn't know what to film first!

At other times it wasn't so pleasant. We had a couple of blizzards which ripped down the radio aerial and cut us off from the nearest centre of civilisation, Resolute, which was over 80 miles away. We managed to fix the aerial, but something even worse happened when I was filming bears in the driving sleet. The wet got into the camera and burnt out the electric motor, which is the first and only time that a camera has broken down on me. Fortunately I had a second camera to complete the sequence.

At least I could see the polar bears and grow accustomed to them. When I came to filming tigers there was little chance of that. Andrew Neal needed a sequence on mangrove swamps for his programme on coastlines, and wanted to get away from the usual species that are featured in such cases – mudskippers, monkeys and other small animals. He had read about the Sundarbans at the mouth of the Ganges in Southern Bangladesh, which is one of the last strongholds of tigers in the world. It is an area of dense mangrove vegetation threaded with muddy channels of water, humid and full of flies. It is also full of beautiful animals such as spotted deer, macaque monkeys, jungle cats, wild pigs and fishing owls.

A room with a view An appropriate cut-out in the privy door – the drop is 600 feet! (*HM*)

Lunchtime in Radstock Bay Seagulls hoping to attend the polar bears' picnic (*NK*)

Then there are the tigers. They wander freely about the Sundarbans and zap people right, left and centre. The north of the swamp is bordered by agricultural land which has a huge population, and the food shortage is so acute that the people keep encroaching into the mangroves (although this is now a national park). Some of their settlements are right next to tiger country and the cattle are a constant source of temptation. Humans are even easier to catch, so they attack them as well. When I went to see the Minister of Forests to thank him for filming permission he said, 'What a shame you will not be here in April when the honey-gatherers have licences to go into the Sundarbans to search for honey. The tigers are very active then.'

Andrew had gone out a few weeks before me to find suitable locations for filming and have platforms built in the trees in areas where tigers were known to be hunting. A Bangladeshi film crew got to hear about this, and decided to go round ahead of us and use all our carefully researched facilities, which was a little sneaky of them. However, they soon had their come-uppance. There was one platform up in the north near the settlements where there are plenty of man-eaters. The Bangladeshis went in there before us, led by one of the park wardens who climbed the platform first. The crew was trudging along behind when suddenly the warden whispered down: 'Don't come any further! There's a tiger stalking you!' The official story is that they spent three days up on the platform waiting for the tiger to show up, but the truth is that they fled in terror and never went near the place again.

On this trip I was accompanied by an old tiger hunter called Ghazi who worked for the government as a ranger and claimed to have killed more than 50 man-eaters. The week before I arrived a tiger had eaten seven villagers, and rangers had tracked and killed it. I was assured that I would be armed and given an experienced guide to look after me, but the only firearm Ghazi had was an old Lee Enfield rifle from the First World War. The barrel was so rusty that if he'd had to fire it at a tiger we would all have been blown up. I made quite a fuss about this and eventually a couple more Lee Enfields were sent down. Until they came all we were armed with was Ghazi's knife, which was a foot long, and a shotgun with one cartridge that wouldn't have much effect on a leaping tiger.

I spent a large part of that trip scared. In the beginning we used the platforms, which were built about 12 feet up in the trees. Ghazi looked at the first one. We didn't know each other's language but I gathered from his expression that he wasn't very happy. After some gesticulation I managed to make out that he didn't think it was high enough and that a tiger could easily have jumped up and got us. We had the platform raised higher, but then discovered that whatever tigers there had been had left the area. So most of the time I just had to crouch in the bushes in a canvas hide filming the deer, monkeys and jungle fowl. It was somewhat distracting sitting in a hide when I knew there were man-eaters around. The local warden cheerfully told me how a fortnight previously a local villager had gone out to collect firewood about 30 yards from his house when a tiger had jumped on his back and dragged him off. That meant that there was definitely one in the vicinity and I was nervous. If I had known how dangerous it was going to be I don't think I would have gone in the first place – perhaps I should have guessed from the speed with which the BBC gave me special life insurance for the trip!

As it turned out, we actually saw little of the tigers. Once I had abandoned the platforms I hired a dug-out canoe and paddled along the creeks looking for footprints in the mud. We saw nothing until one day we spotted a group of deer feeding and decided to film them. One of the boatmen grabbed hold of a mangrove stem but at that moment we heard a snuffling noise in the jungle. Suddenly a female tiger and her cub came out of a bush about 50 yards away. The mother turned and saw us and let out a great roar. The man holding the stem fell into the water with fright, scrambled back into the boat and the rest paddled off frantically. I was angry to miss this perfect opportunity for shooting, and after a lot of shouting I got them to land on the opposite shore, but by that time the tiger had vanished.

This was clearly a place where the animals frequently crossed the creek, so we built a platform in the trees and spent another week watching and waiting. Early one morning we were filming some deer feeding on the opposite bank when suddenly they froze, their tails went up and they looked towards the bushes. The herons and other birds took off and I knew that there must be a tiger approaching. Soon I could hear it moving through the mangroves and I thought 'Got it!' It was only about 20 yards away, but it came right to the edge of the vegetation and no further. I never saw it and that, alas, was the nearest I got to filming a tiger on the entire trip.

Finding wild animals is always a problem, even when there are vast herds of them. Another of my assignments was to film the migration of the caribou across the North American tundra. They set out from their calving grounds in the Arctic Circle in the autumn and travel 600 miles across a huge open space called the Barrens and back south to the forests for the winter. There are thought to be about 130 000 of them so you would think they'd be hard to miss, but it's astonishing how often people set out there and can't find them. We decided to do our research thoroughly and went to see scientists who worked for the Canadian wildlife service. The caribou don't work to

Journey without end The caribou roam the North American tundra and forests all their lives (*S. Roberts/Ardea*)

a strict schedule and the area is so remote that even the experts have only a vague idea of their movements.

However, we listened to their predictions, checked on the maps and settled on a spot to land our Cessna aircraft. We loaded up all our camping gear and food for ten days and flew out over the Barrens. For two hours all we saw was lakes and tundra and I began to get worried. Then at last a trickle of caribou came into sight below, on a trail that went close by a lake. The Cessna was fitted with floats, so we landed on the lake, unloaded the gear, and while the pilot was putting up the tent I was already filming. About a thousand caribou had already gone past, and the main body was on its way – most of them walking close by the tent. For three whole days I filmed as they moved past in their thousands, and then we jumped back into the plane and leapfrogged ahead of them again to try and get more shots in different locations. One afternoon they all holed up on the hilltops to get away from some vicious mosquitoes, so we just settled down to fish: the pilot caught a 12 lb. trout and I had one of 11 lb. In the evening the caribou started off again and we got all the film we wanted, flew back to camp and cooked a memorable supper.

We were also hoping to get some footage of wolves while we were out there, but it was only an outside chance that we would even see any. I actually caught a glimpse of one when we were camping by a ruined barn on some gravel beds. There were grizzly bears on the prowl, so we had sealed all our food in plastic bags to muffle the smell and put it in a box a hundred yards from the tent, with beer cans and bottles on top to give us warning of any intruder. We each kept a rifle by our side in case one or the other of us was attacked in the night. One night I was roused by a strange feeling, as if something were near the tent: if you've been out in the fresh air all day you tend to sleep very soundly, and it takes a lot to wake you up. I peered out and saw a ghostly white shape in the half-light which I recognised as a wolf. It was following the scent of the caribou, looking for any that were injured or lame and could be hunted down. Unfortunately there wasn't enough light for me to use my camera, and that was my only chance because wolves are extremely shy animals.

Sometimes, however, I have a trip where everything goes right after seeming very unpromising at first. Ned Kelly needed a sequence about Himalayan animals to put at the beginning of his programme 'The building of the Earth', to demonstrate the variety of wildlife in mountainous areas. We chose the Everest National Park, which has the highest peaks and deepest valleys in the world but where strangely little is known about the resident species. The region is so vast that

Breakfast on location for Hugh Miles (*HM*)

Your morning call, sir A visitor to the camp in the Himalayas (*HM*)

nobody can give you specific information about where to find particular creatures. I gathered together my gear and some sherpa guides and three weeks' supply of food and set off into the mountains to try and find the animals on Ned's lengthy 'shopping list'. I was very uneasy at first because there was a chance that I might not find half of them. The only thing I could do was talk to everybody I met who could understand English. There were several tourists and climbers in the area and I made a point of stopping and asking if they had seen any mountain goats, musk deer, wolves, yetis and so on during their travels. The sherpas would ask the same thing in the villages we passed through. It was an extraordinarily successful method of instant research, and I managed to find virtually everything that was wanted.

The one creature which remained highly elusive was the blood pheasant. According to all the books I'd read, this bird lived in dense rhododendron forests, preferably near a stream. I had been in every forest on the road and hadn't found anything apart from the odd feather at places where they had been feeding. Then one day we were walking up the side of a mountain and I scanned across the valley with my binoculars. There was a little wood with a stream running through it, and I decided that must be the place. We had to change our itinerary completely so that we could walk for two days up to the head of the valley and back again down the other side. There was no way we could have got there directly. As we approached the wood I hurried ahead of the sherpas, dumped my rucksack and camera gear in a field and went cautiously into the bushes. Straight away I saw a blood pheasant and felt very relieved. By the time I got back to my equipment the sherpas and their yaks had arrived, so we set up camp and in the afternoon I went back to the wood and found – nothing. Still, I knew they were around and sure enough next morning I managed to get some close-up shots of half-a-dozen of them.

My luck held up right to the end of the journey. Communication in the Himalayas is a pretty unreliable business, and as I was heading out of the national park on my way home I received a message from Ned, who had been working with David Attenborough over to the west in the Kali Gandaki Gorge. He had actually sent it off days earlier, hoping that I would read it before I started south again, because it contained a list of eight more species that he wanted me to film. By the time I got it there was no time for me to turn back, but by amazing good fortune I had shot some extra footage of birds and animals, and most of them were on the list. For instance, it had seemed to me that the birds which epitomised the whole park were the alpine chough and the vulture, so I had filmed them. Ned, over 200 miles away, had had the same idea. The mountains must give us telepathic powers.

The cameraman's job is to get the sequences that he is asked for. It costs the BBC thousands of pounds to put you in the Arctic, or in Bangladesh, or up in the Himalayas, and you can only go there once because that is all the budget allows. If you fail, there is going to be a hole in the programme that will have to be filled with library material or something less satisfactory. So you simply have to succeed, and that concentrates the mind wonderfully – especially when time is running out. You focus all your attention on to the subject of the shooting in a way that you could never do if you were just taking happy holiday snaps. The result is that you become extremely sensitive to the way the animals are behaving, and are able to anticipate what they are going to do and get that much closer to them. You have to ignore completely your own human involvement in the scene: you may be hungry, tired, cold, wet and bitten black and blue by mosquitoes but you've got to stay still and fix your whole mind on what is in front of the camera.

I've had an instinctive sympathy with wild animals since I was a lad. I went to the cathedral school in Ely, which is in the Fen country of East Anglia, and soon found that I preferred to spend my time fishing, birdwatching and badger-watching rather than mooching round the town. My hero from an early age was Eric Ashby, 'the silent watcher', whose wonderful television films of wildlife in the New Forest were the result of many hours of painstaking observation and stalking. One programme in particular impressed me: it showed him at work within a few yards of badgers and foxes, and from the moment I saw it I wanted to be a film-maker too. Twenty years later I found myself shooting a film for the BBC about the New Forest and was able to meet him on a couple of occasions. To follow in the footsteps of the Master was an extraordinary sensation.

One of the major secrets of getting good wildlife film is to work alone. In that way you can reduce the disturbance to the animals to a minimum, and if they're not aware of your presence they will behave naturally. Two people add up to far more than twice the disturbance value of a solitary person. By myself, I find that I can often walk right up to an animal, but with someone else that's impossible. The ability to stalk successfully is both a skill you can practise and an instinct you are born with. There is an atmosphere around animals which you can pick up by watching their eyes and ears and tail and sense whether they are relaxed or tense. On many occasions you can work out that there is a predator around even when you can't see one: there may be an alarm call from a bird, or the insects may stop chirring, and you will feel that something is about to happen. If you keep your eyes, ears and nose open you can locate an animal before you actually see it, and this will enable you to set up the camera in the right place and get hidden in good time.

Working alone means of course that I have to lug all my own equipment about. When I'm out on location I carry the tripod and camera on my shoulder all set up so that if something happens suddenly I can put them down and film immediately. To make my silhouette as small as possible I crouch down as I am stalking. When I was filming the caribou there was scarcely any cover to use so I crawled over the tundra pushing my camera in front of me in order to get close enough. I had a haversack at my side full of spare lenses and a rucksack on my back with spare film and maybe a flask of coffee and a sandwich, and with that I could keep going for 12 hours at a stretch. When there are dangerous animals about I have to add a rifle to all that gear. It always gets in the way, sticking up when I am trying to crawl and using up my spare hand; I may be tempted to leave it behind, but I know that the day I do I will be attacked by a grizzly.

However, all your stalking and planning is going to be useless if your camera breaks down at the critical moment. You need equipment that is completely reliable, and I always use the best that money can buy. I've taken it to Everest, Bangladesh, the Arctic and Brazil for this series and the only time it ever broke down was in the extreme conditions of the far north that I mentioned earlier. I also have a big heavy tripod which is half the battle because if it hasn't broken my back by the time I reach the location then I can be sure of getting good steady pictures with clear definition. A robust camera, good lenses and a heavy tripod, all of the highest quality – you don't need anything more sophisticated than that.

Hugh Miles at his happiest Out in the wilderness with his camera (*HM*)

IN THE STUDIO
Macro-photography and other special techniques

Filming animals in a studio is usually described as being done 'under controlled conditions'. As with a lot of wildlife filming, this is rather an overstatement. How much control can you exercise over a rat, a shrew, an electric eel or a greenfly, let alone other creatures which are almost too tiny to see with the naked eye? Quite apart from the erratic behaviour of the animals in his charge, the studio cameraman has to create exactly the right conditions of heat, light and humidity, set up the right surroundings to make them feel at home, give them the right food and cater for any other peculiarities of taste they may have. Instead of simply observing, he has to cosset. On top of this, his filming is being done on such a limited field of vision that he has to be rigorously accurate at all times.

Stephen Bolwell, a freelance cameraman, shot a variety of sequences for *The Living Planet*, beginning in the rudimentary surroundings of a garage in Southampton and progressing to the comparative comfort of a studio in his house. He describes some of the high – and low – spots he encountered:

'I specialise in filming anything from very small insects up to small mammals. Only about half of my work is actually done in the studio: I like to set up situations out of doors as well as get as near to natural conditions as I can. Richard Brock asked me to do some pieces for *The Living Planet* because he knew that I had studied entomology for five years and might be able to help him out with some aspects of insect behaviour.

'Filming in close-up comes under the general heading of macro-photography, and presents a whole set of problems which you don't get in normal shooting. If you've got to focus on something the size of, for example, a mouse's head or smaller, then for a start the lighting requirements are going to be very different. You can't simply reproduce the amount of light that would be present in the wild, because that wouldn't be enough to show up the tiny details. And it is not just the intensity of the lighting that has to be carefully judged but also direction in which it is pointing. A major snag with powerful lighting is that it creates a large amount of heat – often far too much for the little creatures that you are filming. Even if it doesn't fry them, it could well disturb their normal behaviour patterns. So I use fibre optics in many cases when I have to light a small area, because the heat they generate is practically nil. On a big set I will use water-cooled lights which take the heat out of the bulbs.

'Another big problem to overcome is vibration. I like to keep my equipment as simple as possible, otherwise I spend half of my time setting it all up, and the other half tripping over it. Usually I will use a rack fixed on top of the tripod with a head that can be moved backwards and forwards. The secret is to use a really big heavy head so that vibration is cut to a minimum. If the camera is focused on a tiny object, the slightest judder can either put the image out of focus, or lose it altogether. In close-up work any camera movement is exaggerated out of all proportion and the result might well be unusable.

Stephen Bolwell admires the work of a spider in the savannahs of Brazil (*RM/BBC Enterprises*)

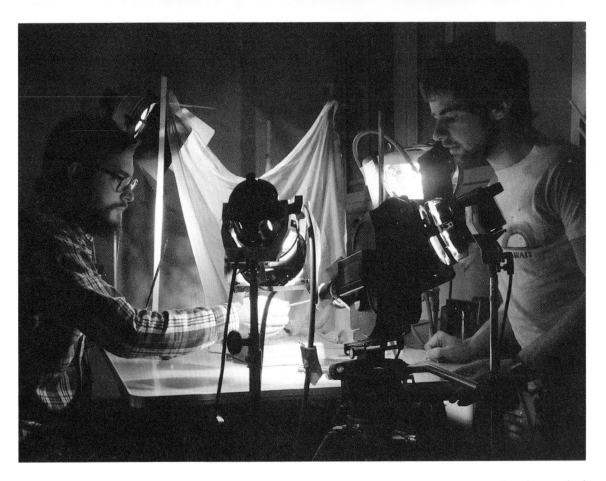

On the bench Stephen Bolwell films in close-up, assisted by a research biologist (*Agilis Pictures*)

'In the studio I use a special macro-bench or a simpler optical bench for filming objects in detail. A macro-bench is so designed that you can move the animal rather than the camera: you put the insect or whatever it is on to the base on the bench and lock the base into position. You focus the camera correctly and start shooting, and if you want to move the animal you press the remote control switch and it moves – forwards, backwards or sideways. It will also rotate, in case you are using a zoom lens. This technique saves you moving the camera, or even touching it in order to re-focus, but it does make lighting difficult. Because the object is moving, even a small distance, the angle of the lighting will alter and maybe fail to show up the details with the same intensity. To overcome this, the lights can be fixed to the base so that they move at exactly the same speed as the object. In my opinion that's a bit of a giveaway, because on the film – if you watch closely – you can see the shadows moving along with the animal, which is hardly natural!

'Of course whether you're using a bench or a bigger set you've also got to take great care not to disturb the animals and interfere with their natural behaviour. For the programme on the northern forests I was asked to film the predation techniques of wood ants. On the face of it, this was a fairly straightforward assignment. All I had to do was go to a patch of coniferous forest, cut off the top of a nest with a shovel (making sure that there are plenty of ants in evidence), take it back to my studio and isolate it on trays. I left them for a few days, feeding them with honey, small insects and maggots until they had established a smaller unit. Once they had settled down I was able to work out their patterns of behaviour – where they dumped their rubbish, where they were feeding and so on. By allowing them to get a little hungry and then providing food I was able to film them carrying off their prey at a set time and place.

'The trouble was that I also wanted to film them foraging for prey up the trunks of trees. They refused to do this correctly in the artificial situation, so I had to go out into the forest again and select another nest. I took a piece of suitably photogenic tree with me and put it close to the nest. Then I put on a very tight set of underclothes, and lay down on top of the nest with my camera, keeping as still as possible so that the ants could get used to this huge obstruction in their midst. They were walking all over me, and didn't take much notice as long as I made no sudden movement. When they did get alarmed they went berserk, sticking their backsides into the air and squirting out formic acid as a means of defence. I was covered in this by the end, and it made me feel so sick that I could hardly drive home afterwards.

Tiny subjects require special techniques This carnivorous caterpillar was shot in Hawaii (*Stephen Bolwell/Agilis Pictures*)

Grass-cutter ants on the march
(*J. Cherrett, Bangor*)

'I had an even more complicated set-up when filming another species of ant – the grass-cutter ants which appeared in the grasslands programme. This creature gnaws down blades of grass, carries them to the nest, cleans them and feeds them to a special fungus: the fungus itself is what the ants eat. The entire process breaks down into a three-act drama – cutting the grass, carrying it back, and feeding the fungus garden – for which three different sets are required. The nest was on a board with glass sides and top, and there was a narrow bridge by which the ants could walk across to another board to collect the grass. All this was placed in trays of water so that the ants couldn't escape. I took some freshly-cut blades of grass and stuck them into a block of oasis (which florists use), arranging it to look as though it stretched away into the distance and that it wasn't really in a studio in England. The ants went out and began cutting the grass: I got shots of that with no trouble. Then they trooped back over the bridge carrying the blades with them.

'Once I had filmed them going into the nest, I then had to show them actually entering from the inside. We had to build another plaster nest with access for the camera, covered in soil so that it looked reasonably natural. The problem here was that the ants did not like the way that the hole was formed, and started altering it, moving the soil and cutting off bits of plaster and generally making a mess. It took a lot of fiddling about to get the entrance satisfactory for them. Finally, I was filming them in the nest. The camera was looking down through a hole in the top, which I had to keep covered with a sheet of glass to maintain the right level of humidity. Of course, the glass became misted up with the hot damp air, and soon made shooting impossible. So I had to take the glass off, but this caused a slight movement of air inside the nest, where the ants are used to everything being perfectly still, so that was another disturbance. Filming something as intricate as this is a matter of solving one problem at a time, and going on until you meet another problem.

'All animals get nervous in artificial conditions, and the bigger they are, the bigger the problems they can cause. Once I was in a studio in Brazil, where a naturalist had a collection of rodents in captivity. It seemed a good opportunity to get some simple footage of each animal by placing them in turn on a studio set and filming their behaviour. The rodents ranged from large rats to small mice, and one by one I picked them up, put them on the set, filmed them, and took them off again. I handled all the mice which were no trouble at all, but I was somewhat apprehensive when it came to the rats.I decided to be bold and start with the biggest, which was about three times the size of a normal British rat, thinking that if I got away with that one the rest would be easier. Gingerly I picked him up and sat him down and he was as good as gold, so I breathed a sigh of relief and turned to the second one (which was only about twice the size of a normal rat). For some reason he got upset and bit me on the hand.

'This didn't seem too dramatic at the time, and I wandered off to find a plaster for the wound. It took a long time to find anyone who spoke English, but eventually I came across a pretty girl who said that she would take me to the medical centre and interpret for me. When the doctor found out that I had been bitten by a rat, he said that I had to have an anti-tetanus injection, which seemed fair enough. He gave me one jab in the arm, then another, and then a third, this time in the stomach. I thought this was a bit odd, and the girl told me that the final jab had been in case of rabies. I would have to have one each day for the next 11 days, and unless I went the full course there was a danger that I would contract the disease and probably die. This was hardly cheering news, especially as I was going off into the bush the next day for a week, out of the reach of any doctor. In the end I had to buy 11 phials of the vaccine and an ice bucket to keep them in, and I had to inject myself once a day. After a week I felt like a drug addict, because I'd run out of places on my stomach to put the needle!

'Most of the animals I handle are completely harmless, but they are all so small that it is easy for them to escape, and this can cause quite a headache, especially if they are loose around the house. One day when I was out, a BBC driver turned up at my parents' house with a box and said "Here are your scorpions." My father lifted the lid, looked inside, and saw a great mass of millipedes, scorpions and other creatures, most of them poisonous. I suppose he's got used to strange things arriving at the door by now. On another occasion I was keeping a pregnant scorpion which I hoped to film as she gave birth. I had to go away for a few days and asked a friend to look after her for me, but when I got back I looked in the box in the airing cupboard and the scorpion had vanished. It had a pretty lethal sting, and I was terrified that it would turn up somewhere unexpected round the house. After two horrendous hours of searching my friend arrived and admitted that the scorpion had actually died in my absence. He had thought it was his fault and had quietly thrown it away somewhere, hoping that I wouldn't notice!

'I was filming a piece for the programme on jungles in which a snake has a confrontation with a stick insect, and both these creatures were in the house. Just as I had taken the lid off the snake's tank one day the telephone rang, and I dashed out without replacing the lid. The snake disappeared, and I had to take the whole room apart to find it again: eventually I discovered it underneath the carpet. The stick insects were always getting out as well, which wasn't so worrying because they're not dangerous. However, they can give you quite a shock if you tread on one, as my father found out when he was on his way to the bathroom one night. In the dark he put his bare foot on a great spiky stick insect and nearly had a heart atack. These sorts of incidents are going on all the time. I shot some sequences for the final programme in the series, about the species of animal that you find in an ordinary house, and I've still got the woodworm, cockroaches and death-watch beetle to prove it. I think the mice have all gone now.

'Altogether I am forced to live a rather eccentric life at times. I had to get some film of a shrew, which was a big problem because you can only keep shrews in captivity for a very short time. They are extremely nervous creatures and take a long time to get used to captive conditions, so you have to spend as long as possible in their company for them to lose some of their fear of you. It seemed to me that the best way to do this was to have the shrew in its glass tank right next to my bed. The base of the tank was made of plaster, and one of the sides slid up so that food could be placed in it. The first shrew I had eventually came to accept me and the filming was going along nicely until the poor animal died. I started it all again with a second shrew, but this one quickly discovered that it could chew its way through the plaster base and escape. Once it was out it was difficult to catch, because being so small it could nip under doors and couldn't be isolated in one room. I decided that the only thing to do was to put some food in the tank, leave the side open, turn out the light and wait for the shrew to turn up. As soon as I heard it in the tank I would slam the side down and bash on the light, but every time the shrew managed to run out first. I put down live traps, but the shrew jumped over the trip bars and avoided setting them off. After about four hours of this I thought that I'd just give up and get some sleep. I turned off the light and lay down and then suddenly I felt this little body moving about, half-way down the bed. It ran out over the pillow, and after that I had no chance of getting to sleep, so I spent another couple of hours chasing it round the room until, at about 5 o'clock in the morning, I caught it at last.'

Each studio film-maker develops his own specialised techniques. Yet so wide is the range of facilities required for this increasingly cunning and complex branch of photography that a whole complex of studios may need to be set up. London Scientific Films is run by several young cameramen, each of whom works in his own studio but also has access to a large amount of sophisticated equipment. Together they filmed several of the close-up sequences for Richard Brock's programme 'Sweet fresh water'. Animal behaviour underwater is, naturally enough, difficult to photograph satisfactorily in the wild, and so any film with rivers as its central subject is bound to depend heavily on artificial situations. But how do you go about simulating the flow of a river inside a small studio in North London? Alasdair MacEwen and Martyn Colbeck of London Scientific explain how they tackled it:

'The most difficult part of creating an artificial piece of river is fixing exactly the correct speed of flow of the water. You have to cut out as much turbulence as possible, particularly if you are photographing very small creatures. The turbulence will cause them to bob about in and out of the camera frame and make filming impossible. What you have to create is called laminar flow – a smooth passage of water in which there is little or no turbulence. What we used was a reservoir of water flowing into a rectangular tank which had a shelf in it. The water came in at the bottom under pressure, curved round the edge of the shelf, and passed out across the top of the shelf, which was covered in stones and weed and sand to make it look natural. By the time the water reached the top of the shelf all the turbulence had been got rid of, and it ended up as laminar flow. Inside this apparatus we wanted to be able to film the ways in which caddis fly and blackfly larvae have adapted to living in fast-flowing rivers. The blackfly larva anchors itself to a pebble and puts out a special fan to collect the particles of food as they pass through the water. Once we had smoothed out the flow, we were able to shoot this satisfactorily.

'After that we filmed the caseless caddis fly larva in the same tank. This species is native to Britain and it builds a web in which it catches the bits and pieces flowing down the river. We filmed the whole procedure of this web-building right from the beginning, with the larva laying down the main strands and then putting cross-strands in. To give a story to the sequence, we showed that amongst the food caught in the web can be the blackfly larvae that had been seen before. The larvae can get swept from their foothold on a pebble and swirled downstream as prey for the bigger caddis fly larva. It was actually quite difficult to release a blackfly larva in just the right spot so that it would be caught in the net in a convincing and natural way.

'To try and get insects and other tiny animals to do something specific in a short time is always a problem. They won't behave to order, and if you don't give them exactly the right conditions they may not perform at all. You also have such powerful lights on them in the studio that if, for example, you put down a greenfly and wait to film it taking off, it can be touch and go whether the thing takes

The ocean in Oxford A specially-constructed model of the Pacific seafloor being set up by Oxford Scientific Films (*P. K. Sharpe/Oxford Scientific films*)

off or is fried first. We do of course keep the lights as far away as possible so as to avoid as much distress to the insect as we can. On top of all this in such close-up work you have an absolutely minimal depth of field, and if the insect takes off in any other direction than the one you want then you've had it. You can go on filming for hours and the right sequence never comes up. Already in your mind you can envisage ringing up the BBC and saying "We've used 20 rolls of film and we haven't got anything yet!" Because a lot of insect behaviour has to be shown in slow-motion, you have to be shooting at high speed. There was one particular occasion when we were filming a butterfly taking off, and the camera was set to expose 2000 frames per second (making it 80 times slower than normal). We switched on the lights and the camera at the same time, the film whizzed through and we thought we had got it. But when the film was processed we found that the butterfly didn't actually take off until the last few frames of the roll.

'All we can do is go on trying until we get the right footage. For the programme "Sweet fresh water" we wanted to film an electric eel catching a fish by stunning it with an electrical discharge. The specimen we used had been kept in a tank in Sheffield for several months. Over that time it had come to feed regularly, and we were assured that you just had to pop a fish into the tank and the eel would take it. Martyn was despatched up north to film it, and started setting up his equipment on a Monday. Tuesday and Wednesday and

(Left) Simulating an underwater earthquake. (Right) The Galactoscope – a snorkel camera designed to film inside the model of the Marianas Trench (*P. K. Sharpe/Oxford Scientific Films*)

Thursday came and went and nothing happened – the electric eel didn't want to know. Friday was the last day of the shoot, and Martyn was becoming increasingly despondent. In despair he phoned Alasdair in London and told him the bad news; Alasdair rang up the BBC and told them. Meanwhile Martyn had gone back to his camera for one last attempt before packing up. Lo and behold, he sat down and the eel did its party piece as if by magic. After five days of waiting, the whole thing was over in barely a couple of minutes. The fish swam up, the eel came out of his lair, shocked the fish, caught it in his mouth and then went into a huge frenzy of activity, thrashing around and sending up clouds of silt and rubbish. Martyn thought it was all over, when the eel suddenly appeared at the side of the tank again and let the fish go. This was a nice ending for the fish and the cameraman, because he shot a tailpiece of the fish swimming drunkenly away with teethmarks on its flanks.

'This incident illustrates perfectly one of the unwritten laws of our sort of filming: things only happen when the cameraman has left the studio! You can do as much research as you like into a subject and talk to as many experts as possible, but in the end you just have to sit and watch your specimen. The demands of close-up photography are significantly different from those of scientific research, and you find that nine times out of ten even the experts have not watched those animals as closely as you are going to. If you want to know to within the nearest hour or two when a fly is going to emerge from its pupa or lay its eggs, you simply have to wait and concentrate behind your camera. The actual rolling of the film takes up very little time indeed.

'Academic biologists will often try to be as helpful as they can, but they can find it hard to appreciate just how accurate our work has to be. For instance, we were asked to see if it was possible to film greenfly in flight for the programme "The sky above". This – if it could be done at all – would have to be shot in a wind tunnel, where the aphids, though flying, might be kept in a stationary position. Imperial College in London generously offered us the use of the wind tunnel at their Research Station. This had been specially built to monitor the behaviour of greenfly, who at a certain time of the year are attracted to the colour blue. They climb to the top of whatever plant they are on, take off and fly up towards the blue of the sky. The wind tunnel had a blue top which attracted the aphids, but it also pushed down air against them, effectively keeping them in the same place. The college also provided us with one of their researchers to drive the contraption, who was greatly skilled in controlling these greenfly and keeping them static. On the face of it this sounded perfect, but we soon realised that their idea of stationary was rather different from ours. In order to maintain the insects in the frame for us they would have had to have held them in a band of roughly an inch in height by half an inch in width, and this was clearly beyond that wind tunnel – or any other machine for that matter.'

The smaller the animal, the less margin there is for error. One slight judder of the camera lens may not be noticeable when it is focused on a gorilla, but a tiny insect will be lost from view entirely. The BBC in Bristol experienced this sort of problem for the first time during the making of *The Living Planet*. After using other people's macro-benches for years, the Natural History Unit eventually persuaded the powers that be to provide them with their own. It was built to incorporate all the best features from other benches and, with a magnification range down from 22 times, it was intended for beetles, insects and seeds rather than microbes. The specimen in view could be manipulated in a number of different directions, and when some complicated set of manoeuvres was required a computer could be connected up. The computer would 'watch' the cameraman going through the moves in slow time and then repeat them exactly at the required speed.

Ian Calvert, who directed the programme on northern forests, was among the first to make use of the new bench:

'We decided to use this macro-bench for filming the community of incredibly small creatures which lives amongst the leaf litter on the floors of the temperate forests. Numerically this community is very large – countless millions of animals – and biologically it is very important because the whole forest depends on it to help break down the leaves and recycle the nutrients at the end of each growing season. Without these the trees would not be provided with the minerals to grow and pump water up into their trunks. They are easy enough to find, and all I had to do was go out into the woods, collect a big pile of leaves and put it through a sieve. Once I had got down to the finer grain of litter I could see the insects, but if there was any difficulty I could simply place it under a strong light: they will migrate away from the light right down to the bottom of the litter, out through the sieve and on to a white dish, where they can be easily spotted and picked up.

'The problems of filming things the size of a pinhead are quite horrendous. You are often working with a depth of field which might be one sixteenth of an inch, and you have to work out exactly how deep your field is for the size of magnifcation needed. And in order to get a good depth you need a lot of light. At the same time the more light you put on one small spot the hotter the creature will get, and insects are very susceptible to heat: you have to maintain a balance all the time between having enough light to obtain a decent depth of field and keeping them alive. This was all complicated by the fact that we wanted to film some of the animals actually moving. There is a kind of Serengeti in miniature down there in the leaf litter. The box mites and springtails are fairly static because they are herbivores and simply chew at the leaves, breaking them up into small pieces, and then the bacteria get to work on them. They are preyed on by much bigger animals called pseudo-scorpions which, when they are magnified by the camera lens, look like real science fiction monsters with two large claws and huge mouth parts.

'One piece of action that we wanted to shoot was the moment when a pseudo-scorpion catches a springtail. This is a quite horrific process: the pseudo-scorpion grabs hold of the springtail and uses its front claws to bash its brain out; then it sucks the animal dry from the head downwards. This sequence lasts about 30 seconds in the programme but it took us about five days to get it right. It took so long because we had to have everything happening within a very narrowly defined area. The pseudo-scorpion was supposed to sit still, then the springtail had to approach it, get caught and eaten, and this all had to occur on the spot where the camera was focused. It was no use if the pseudo-scorpion moved sideways even a sixteenth of an inch in order to grab its prey. The only way to get round the problem was to set up the situation time after time and keep patiently trying until we got the sequence that we wanted. An additional difficulty lay in handling these tiny creatures and putting them where we wanted without damaging them. They are so fine that we could not use tweezers or anything like that. What I did in the end was to pull out one of my own eyelashes, cement it to the end of a toothpick and then just spit on the end of the eyelash. The saliva was sticky enough to adhere to the insect so that we could pick it up and place it in the correct position. As it dries off under the warmth of the lights, the insect becomes free and can walk off again. Then of course you have to keep all these creatures in one small area, because they could easily wander off and disappear into the woodwork. We built little islands of soil and silicone sealant and surrounded them with water, which stopped the animals escaping and helped to keep the atmosphere humid.'

Television viewers have become so accustomed over the years to watching the dramatic results of such specialised and intricate photography that they may tend to take it all for granted. Greatly speeded-up sequences using time-lapse cameras, for example, have almost lost their capacity to startle, but this does not make the technical achievement any the less remarkable. The opening of the weird rafflesia flower in a tropical rainforest was filmed on location in Indonesia by freelance film-makers Jim Frazier and Densey Clyne. The shooting had to take place continuously over a number of days, so a permanent lighting rig had to be set up to give a constant and uniform light, even at night. Then, because of the possibility of tropical rainstorms, the whole apparatus had to be covered in a tarpaulin shelter. But it finally worked.

Stephen Bolwell tackled another important time-lapse sequence – the growth of a fungus from amid the debris on a forest floor:

'I couldn't just take a camera out into the woods and film these fungi, because they were growing at night, and artificial lighting over a period of three or four days becomes impossibly expensive. Also I had to take great care to light them evenly on both sides: if I had put all the light on one side, they would have grown towards that light and gone crooked. Then of course I could never be sure exactly when the fungus was going to start growing. You are supposed to be able to predict this by spotting the moment when the top has bulged to a certain size: things can start moving quite fast after that. Alternatively, it might be a false alarm, and I will have had the camera running for five hours, exposing one frame every ten seconds, with nothing to show for it. The shooting of this sequence actually took me more than a month, and it was murder. I was busy with other

The World's biggest flower The opening of the rafflesia, filmed with a time-lapse camera in Indonesia by Jim Frazier (*Densey Clyne*)

projects during the day, but every four hours I had to go and check the fungus for signs of action. At night I would set my alarm, go to bed at about midnight, get up at 3 o'clock and again at 6 o'clock to make sure that I wasn't missing anything. Doing that for five weeks was absolutely exhausting.'

The difficulty of lighting a time-lapse subject evenly over a period of days is one to which the technicians of London Scientific Films gave a great deal of attention. Tim Chard explains how the newly devised system was given a rather premature baptism:

'Most specialist film-makers have time-lapse units which they can use. You can either rig up the camera so that you can shoot in sunshine

The experimental time-lapse camera system, suspended over a giant waterlily at Kew Gardens (*London Scientific Films Ltd*)

or daylight, using the normal mechanism on a reasonably short-term time-lapse such as ten frames an hour, or you can go for a longer-term shoot which requires the use of special shutters and cold lighting conditions. We developed a system which allowed us to flood a specific area – about eight square feet – with artificial light. So, even if we were filming over a long period in conditions which varied from bright sunshine to night-time darkness, we could maintain an absolutely constant level of light, frame by frame. Using this system we were able to tackle certain subjects which it would be very difficult to set up in a studio.

'One such was the giant waterlily which I shot in one of the large greenhouses at Kew for the programme on rivers and lakes ("Sweet fresh water"). We were actually still at the prototype stage with the system when Richard Brock asked us to film the lily, and were a little unsure about putting it to the test so early on. But Richard stressed that this flowering sequence had to be shot that year, so we just had to go ahead and try it. We went down to Kew Gardens and built a scaffolding tower in the middle of the greenhouse, right over the pond which had the giant lily in it. Inside the tower we set up the time-lapse camera and the lighting equipment and got it going. But the trouble with prototypes is that something is almost bound to go wrong. The greenhouse was a tropical one, with artificial conditions of 90 per cent humidity and temperatures up in the 80s, and our delicate equipment was just sitting there stewing. I was filming on another assignment as well which involved a lot of travelling around, so I would get up at 5 o'clock every morning, drive down to Kew to check the time-lapse equipment and then go off and shoot for the other programme. Throughout the day the people at Kew would phone me up with news that the camera was not firing or some other hitch. One particular gremlin kept affecting the circuit breakers which they have to have fitted for safety reasons in their greenhouses because of the water and high humidity. The camera regularly tripped all the circuit breakers in the place and shut down all the electricity, which made us none too popular at the time! We had three or four false starts, but eventually we got the sequence.'

When shooting of a particular species is over, the film has been developed and the set packed away, there often remains one unlooked-for problem. What are the cameramen going to do with the animals afterwards? Alasdair MacEwen has found that this is more complicated than it may seem:

'The trouble is that most of these creatures have got used to a life of luxury and ease while they are in the studio. If they are native to this country, then you can release them to the great outdoors again, but with things like tropical fish you have no choice but to keep them as pets. We still have fish here that we filmed over two years ago and, far from dying off gracefully, they have got so acclimatised that they are breeding like crazy. Any offer of a good home is gratefully accepted.'

STUNTS AND SPECIAL EFFECTS

David Attenborough wrote himself into some fairly hair-raising corners during the making of *The Living Planet*. He is well accustomed to handling animals which are potentially dangerous – indeed the public seems to expect it of him – and sequences such as those which showed him swimming among sharks, sticking his head into the nest of a great grey owl and standing within paw-stretch of a hibernating black bear are obtained strictly within the limits of personal safety. However, not content with this, he also exposed himself to some of the most extreme conditions to be found on Earth, walking through Death Valley at noon, standing next to an active volcano, and heading out into the vast emptiness of the Indian Ocean in search of a tiny group of islands. At times, and most dramatically of all, he even left the safety of the Earth's surface. In 'Jungle', he strapped on a climbing harness and hauled his way 200 feet up into a giant kapok tree. In 'The sky above', he bounced around weightless inside a plummeting Boeing 707 and ascended high into the atmosphere in a hot-air balloon.

It is all too easy for the viewer to forget that there has to be someone on the other side of the camera as well. The cameraman also has to swim with the sharks, suffer the desert heat and bounce around in the sky. Actually getting the camera into the right position is in many cases more complicated and arduous than getting the narrator there. How, for example, did the ropes with their labour-saving Jumar ratchet climbing system come to be hanging from a tree branch as high as a cathedral spire? The answer is, of course, that someone had to clamber up and fix them, and that someone was Adrian Warren, the producer of the programme:

'The first problem you find in climbing a jungle tree is that there are no low branches for you to start on. The first limb can be about 90 feet up, and until that the trunk is sheer, without a handhold of any kind. I solved that by selecting a good thick vine which was dangling down and shinning up it Tarzan-style as far as I could go. From there I transferred to the top of a small tree (90 feet is very small in a tropical forest!) and threw a stick with a line attached over the lowest branch of the kapok tree. I had to make several attempts at this, because the stick had to be far enough clear to weigh down the line and carry it all the way to the ground. Once that was done, I climbed down again myself, attached the main rope to the end of the line, pulled on the stick until the main rope was all the way up over the branch and down to the ground again, and tied it to a handy root. The rope was now doubled, so I could fix on the Jumar handles, and these made the next ascent a great deal easier.

'Up on the branch again I encountered another unusual problem – the undergrowth. The branches of tropical forest trees are an entirely separate habitat from that down on the ground, and support a whole community of profusely flowering plants such as bromeliads and epiphytes of various sorts. I had to scramble thigh-deep through this vegetation and then throw the stick with the attached line once more, as high as it would go. This process was repeated until I had got the ropes fixed at the required height: it was actually so high that I had to tie two lengths together. The whole thing took me a day to set up, and then I had to teach David how to use it. He had done some rock-climbing about 30 years previously, he told me, but nothing since. He got up there well enough – the trouble was that he had to transfer from the Jumars and come down again, which took rather longer!'

It may have been a tough haul for Messrs Attenborough and Warren, but how can a cameraman shoot film from the same vantage point? With both hands needed to operate his camera, he could not manoeuvre himself up or down, yet the programme features some breathtaking shots from various heights in the forest canopy. The purpose of David Attenborough's climb was to examine the three different layers of habitat in the jungle – the twilit and largely bare forest floor, the empty airspace above, and the lush foliage of the tree crowns above that. Until recently, little was known of the life that swarmed up in the leaves of the canopy because no one could get up

A long haul Dicky Bird records, Hugh Maynard films, Adrian Warren directs and David Attenborough climbs (*RB*)

there. Now, however, many mountain-climbing techniques have been adapted to help gain access to these vertiginous regions, and film-makers have not been slow to exploit this. Neil Rettig, for one, had been experimenting with the use of ropes and pulleys in his shooting for several years. While filming in Costa Rica for *The Living Planet*, he and Adrian Warren perfected a complex procedure for taking vertical tracking shots which started at ground level, rose up through the leaves, and ended up in the crown of the tree. Adrian Warren explains how it was done:

'Neil must take most of the credit for thinking out this method of filming, because he did most of the work on it and got me interested in climbing trees in the first place. We started off with the cameraman – Neil – simply fixing a rope in a figure-of-eight clip, launching himself off the branch and abseiling down, shooting as he came. The drawback with this was that after about 20 feet he started to twist and it was impossible to keep the camera steady. So we had to devise a way of getting a steadier and more even descent using a pulley with a counterweight on the other end of the rope from the cameraman. In the end we did it like this: we climbed the tree using a climbing belt and found a suitable horizontal branch to which we fixed two pulleys ten feet apart. Then we threaded a 200-foot-long manila rope through the pulleys: Neil fixed himself on one end, and I fixed myself on the other to act as the human ballast system. Neil also had guide ropes on either side of him which were stretched from the branch to the ground and were attached to his waist with carabiners, and these prevented him from twisting as he went down. He started at the top and I at the bottom and, because his camera made him rather heavier than me, I had to have a guide rope as well so that I could control the speed of the descent with my hands.

'After that was working satisfactorily, we took on a much more formidable challenge – horizontal tracking shots high up across the top of the canopy itself. This was the natural progression from something we had tried to do in Borneo in order to get a view of a flying squirrel, keeping track with it as it glided. We had stretched a steel wire across a gap of 50 yards between two trees, slightly sloping so that a camera could slide down under its own momentum on a pulley. After testing the rig with a bag of stones to try and make sure that the camera would brake naturally before hitting the tree, we tied a small camera on and launched it down the wire. It whizzed down but the braking system failed and I had to watch it whack into the tree. The film we got from that shows a head-on crash and splinters of wood flying about! I dug out a perfectly disc-shaped piece of bark from the lens.

'This was not too encouraging, but we were resigned to the fact that fantastic ideas that are worked out on paper never quite seem the same when you get on location. The effect we wanted to obtain was of floating over the great unbroken canopy of leaves like a big bird of prey, pointing out the contrast between that and the dim, humid world below the foliage. At first we thought it would be fairly simple to set up, but you just try finding two forest trees of similar heights that are between 200 and 300 feet apart! And once we had found them, we had somehow to get a line between the two at a height of about 150 feet. The jungle is so overgrown that we would have had to hack our way through if we wanted to carry the line on foot from one tree to the other, and even then we would have had to hoist it up through the impenetrable tangle of lianas and fig vines and bromeliads and so on. The only solution was for us to climb each tree in turn with a crossbow and fire a bolt with a light line attached as far as it would go, then find the two lines and tie them together. In theory this was fine, but in practice the lines fell short of each other by about 20 yards. We had to scramble about in the tangled lianas trying to find them and bring them together. All this took us about three days.

'Eventually we did it and had the line stretched as taut as possible across this yawning gap. All we needed then was the courage to launch ourselves out across it. The dangers were considerable, because by stretching a rope that tight we were using up about 15 per cent of its breaking strain, and if the pulley started running off centre it might fray it and weaken it still further. But, on the other hand, it had to be as taut as a guitar string so that the cameraman would be able to slide along as evenly as possible. Even at that tension, the trees themselves bent a little as soon as he started off, and by the time he was three quarters of the way across he was going uphill and then stopping altogether, well short of the other tree. However, we had another line attached by which he could be pulled back by me.

'This short account misses out most of the sweat and hard work we got through. Our clothes were full of ants and all sorts of rubbish

Neil Rettig, 150 feet up in the Costa Rican jungle, checks his life-lines (*AW*)

kept falling down from above as we climbed. The rope was slippery, our hands were wet with perspiration, and both we and the line were continually getting caught up in the foliage. Jungle trees may look massive and strong, but they tend to shed their branches as easily as English trees shed their leaves: the weight of the vines and other vegetation becomes too much for them to bear. Then of course there were various insects and other creatures that we had to beware of. As we were in the process of doing a vertical shot, I happened to glance at Neil – him on his way down and me on my way up – when I saw a scorpion land on his neck and crawl inside his collar. I didn't want to make him jump so I called out quietly to him, telling him to take his jacket off. He was at that moment 50 feet above the ground, but he managed to get it off and shake the scorpion out.'

Adrian Warren is never happier than when suspended somewhere in the sky, whether it is by parachute or simply in the cockpit of an aircraft. It was this enthusiasm for all things aerial which made him the obvious choice as director of the programme 'The sky above'. Many of the original ideas were in fact his own, though not all of these found favour with David Attenborough, who regretfully turned down the suggestion that he should be filmed speaking part of his commentary during a free-fall skydive! One highly effective stunt that was taken up involved the narrator in marginally less discomfort, and graphically demonstrated the importance that the force of gravity plays in our lives. Adrian Warren recalled that American astronauts in training are given experience of weightless conditions by being taken up in a specially adapted jet airliner to 36 000 feet. At that height the pilot puts the plane into a rapid dive, and for a short period the pull of gravity is negated. He investigated further:

'I got in touch with the National Aeronautics and Space Administration (NASA) at Houston in Texas, and after much discussion they were happy to give us a number of trips in their zero-gravity jet. They were making regular training flights and had room in the aircraft for our crew. Their only stipulation was that we all passed a stringent medical test before we went up, to make sure that we could stand what they called the "violent flight profile" without cracking up. The RAF agreed to give us the tests, which turned out to be a lot more unpleasant than the eventual flight. We were put into a vacuum chamber which simulated the air pressure at 4500 feet. Next to it was another chamber in which was simulated the air pressure at 60 000 feet. Then the valve between the two was opened and there was a sudden fall in pressure which literally sucked the air out of us (we had been advised to keep off baked beans for a day or so before!) This test showed the effects of the explosive decompression that would occur

A sideways look Adrian Warren having fun, thanks to NASA

if a door or a window blew out of the plane.

'Filming under these conditions gave us several unique problems. The jet – a military version of the Boeing 707 with specially padded walls – began by zooming up to 36 000 feet, which produced double-gravity and stuck us all firmly to the floor. Then the pilot pulled back the throttle and the aircraft belly-flopped, producing a period of zero-gravity which lasted for 30 seconds. This was a short enough time in which to get any satisfactory film at all, but we had the added complication of needing David Attenborough to rise weightless from the floor at exactly the right moment. He had to speak some introductory words as he sat cross-legged on the floor, and then rise gracefully towards the ceiling. Synchronising this with the pilot's parabola was quite a headache, especially when Martin Saunders the cameraman was floating about as well, and in all it took us 14 attempts.

'NASA gave us three days of flying, which worked out at six hours in the air and 120 parabolas. Being jolted around 40 times a day over the Gulf of Mexico did terrible things to our internal organs, I'm sure, and we were regularly being checked for signs of air sickness. It's no wonder they refer to the aircraft as "The Vomit Comet"! Added to that were the various bumps and bruises we received as we

floated helplessly about the cabin. When the pilot pulled out of his speed dive and normal gravity was restored, we were all likely to be stuck like flies to the ceiling, and would hit the deck with quite a whack.'

Gravity and the problems presented by it were at the heart of the programme on the skies. After demonstrating in dramatic fashion what would happen to us without the power of gravity, David Attenborough moved on to consider how various plants and animals become airborne and move in the air. Passive fliers, such as pollen seeds and fungal spores, are simply caught by the wind and transported wherever it blows. But when a seed develops an aero-foil, as the sycamore seed has done, then it can make use of it to help in dispersal even when there is no wind. Photographing the rotary movement of such seeds was no easy matter but Adrian Warren, with the expert help of researcher Keith Scholey, designed a wind tunnel specially for the purpose, and this was built in the BBC workshops. By carefully controlling the speed of the wind they were able to keep the spinning seeds in one place, and by rolling behind them a background of painted sky they were able to give an impression of actual movement. The tunnel came remarkably cheap at £1000, and is now a permanent piece of Natural History Unit apparatus.

From seeds, the programme's attention moved further from ground level to the active fliers – insects, gliding reptiles and birds. Birds are probably the most frequently filmed creatures in the natural world, and it is hard to think of any spectacularly original way of portraying them. Would it be possible, wondered the producers, to obtain a long tracking shot of a bird in flight, giving the viewer the illusion that he was travelling alongside it? Slowly, a plan took shape, based on the famous researches of biologist Konrad Lorenz. A brood of day-old red-breasted goslings was put into the care of Rose Eastman, wife of BBC cameraman Ron Eastman. The orphans quickly adopted Rose as their mother, imprinting on their minds the sight of her bright red wellington boots and the sound of her voice. As they grew up, they began to follow her – or rather her boots – everywhere. To encourage them to fly, she pedalled across fields on her bicycle, and the geese flapped along easily beside her. At last came the ultimate test. With Ron Eastman and his camera balanced precariously in the boot and Rose in the passenger seat dangling her boots and shouting encouragement, Beth Huntley drove her sports car along a straight and unobstructed piece of road. The geese obediently followed, flying alongside the car at speeds of up to 60 mph and the resulting film, shown in slow motion, was one of the most intimate portraits of a bird in flight ever shot.

Higher still were the realms of the huge soaring birds such as the albatross, the condor and the lammergeier (a bearded vulture). At levels beyond that even these magnificent creatures are unable to fly, but there is still life to be found. The question was: how could a camera be taken up that high? Once again, Adrian Warren's aeronautical interests provided the answer, and he plumped for a hot-air balloon. This was perhaps the most ambitious of all the stunts inspired by the programme, and was certainly the most complex to organise, but it served to solve two problems at once. The first concerned filming at all at such an inhospitable height; the second concerned the presence of David Attenborough. To give a consistent shape to each programme, the producer had to feature the great man in person at reasonably regular intervals. This was a straightforward matter when he was dealing with largely earthbound topics such as the world's deserts or temperate forests, because he could be filmed striding through the landscape, climbing trees or looking at animals in many different permutations. But 'The sky above' was almost exclusively about airborne things, and so the narrator obviously had to become airborne as well. A hot-air balloon was the perfect vehicle.

The whole enterprise, however, took a vast amount of patient planning and waiting before it got off the ground. Adrian Warren's first task was to find a balloon of the right size:

'Because this was to be a sync filming trip, we needed to be able to cram a minimum of five people into the balloon basket – David Attenborough, myself, the pilot, Martin Saunders and Dicky Bird. Initially we thought we might have to take a doctor as well in case of emergency, but managed to do without him in the end. Then there was the camera and the sound recording equipment, not to mention a specially fitted oxygen console, with cylinders and breathing apparatus, which we would need when the air became unbearably thin at about 15 000 feet, and the bulky parachutes. I discovered that there were only two balloons in the world which would be big enough to take all this weight (and size) up to the altitude we wanted to reach. One of these was so big that it would have been impracticable to use: the larger the balloon, the more unstable it becomes, and the weather conditions have to be increasingly gentle. Eventually we hired one which was five times the size of a normal balloon. It had been built for Don Cameron, who was at that time practising to use it for a round-the-world expedition.

'The next step was for us all to be given high-altitude training by the RAF. They had agreed to help us, but had limited us to 25 000 feet: above that height you have to wear a partial-pressure suit and pre-breathe pure oxygen in order to purge the nitrogen from your system and prevent yourself getting the bends. We were put into a vacuum chamber which simulated the experience of hypoxia at that height, and were then told to take our oxygen masks off and do a series of simple tasks, such as reciting a nursery rhyme or writing the alphabet backwards. We were perfectly all right for a couple of minutes and then we found ourselves starting to get silly. It was rather like being drunk, in that we didn't know how silly we were getting. But it was valuable to gain experience of this sort, because as the brain becomes starved of oxygen it becomes less efficient without you being aware of the fact. Once you know how badly the thinness of the air can affect you, you can at least make some allowance for it.'

Meanwhile Andrew Buchanan was getting his teeth into the logistical details, trying to do the thinking for everybody just in case they forgot anything:

'Adrian and I worked for four weeks non-stop on the balloon project, and had no time for any other work. The details we had to go into were endless. What weather conditions did we need? Where could we make the ascent from? Where did we get the correct equipment from, and how long did we need to hire it for? Did we require special flight clearance from the Civil Aviation Authority? Would the equipment work once we had got it up there? Would the batteries hold their charge, and should the camera spindles be lubricated with low temperature grease? (That was, of course, the cameraman's business, but it was a question I had to ask because he wasn't around during the planning stage.) Then, once the flight was over, how did the people on the ground find out where the balloon had got to?

'The single most important factor was the weather. We had to find an area of high pressure so that the balloon could ascend easily, but one free from high winds. At 25 000 feet you can hit some very strong winds which could blow you miles out over the North Sea in no time, so you have to take enormous care in picking exactly the right sort of conditions and launching site. We selected a number of possible sites by consulting with the Meteorological Office in London and working out wind directions at certain times. After the number of sites had been narrowed down to five, we set up a telephone network through which everybody who was involved in the project could be told where to go and at what time. Naturally enough, most of these sites were in the Bristol area – one on the coast, one down in Wiltshire, and one in north Gloucestershire – but the weather was so terrible over the fortnight we had set aside for filming that they all had to be abandoned. So at a few hours' notice we had to find

an alternative site way up in Perthshire, get new flight clearances, and roust everybody out of their beds, into cars and on the road to Scotland.'

Altogether 18 people assembled on the Perthshire hillside that morning at 5 o'clock. Apart from the five in the main balloon, there was a crew of three in a second 'chase' balloon which included a cameraman who would take film of the first stage of the ascent. On the ground was an assistant cameraman who was to shoot the whole proceedings, plus RAF personnel to monitor events and ground crews

Will it all fit? Cameraman, recordist, director, narrator and pilot had to cram themselves and their equipment into the basket of the hot-air balloon. Oxygen masks were essential for the high-altitude work (*RM/BBC Enterprises*)

with cars who would chase the balloons around the countryside as best they could. After a perfect take-off, both balloons floated up into the clear early morning sky, but it was soon apparent that the main craft was gaining height much more quickly than its chaser. Eventually a layer of cloud came across, and it was lost from sight. To their dismay, the watchers on the ground discovered that the radio intercom system that had been rigged up to keep them in contact with the two balloons had broken down, so they had to rely on the RAF radar for information of where they were headed.

Meanwhile, in the increasingly thin atmosphere above the cover of the clouds, everything was going according to plan aboard the main balloon. Various ingenious devices had been set up, including a home-made aerial plankton collector. This was simply a metal box with a fan inside it and a tube with a funnel on one end covered in fine-mesh net. The idea was for David Attenborough to lower this contraption over the side of the balloon once they had reached about 15 000 feet; the fan would suck in any particles of life that might be floating around at that forbidding altitude, and they would get caught on the netting. The point of this exercise was to demonstrate how tiny aphids and other insects could be blown up by air currents, travel many miles and survive the experience. Unfortunately, when David Attenborough hauled the collector in, it was found to have caught nothing at all, a fact he was honest enough to explain on film. However, he was able to produce instead a jar of samples which had been gathered earlier.

Most of the filming was done by Martin Saunders, perched precariously on the edge of the basket. But Adrian Warren also wanted to obtain some exterior shots of the balloon, and had rigged up a Heath-Robinsonish camera system which was suspended from the envelope itself. Two cine cameras – one with a telephoto lens and one with a wide-angle lens – and one still camera were mounted inside an insulated picnic box, each of them operated by radio control from the balloon. The box was hung by rope from a pulley on the very top of the hot-air envelope, the bulge of the envelope carrying it about 30 feet clear of the side of the basket. The height of the box could be adjusted to make sure that the people in the balloon were in the centre of the camera frame, and for this purpose, Adrian Warren had fixed the inner tube of a toilet roll on to the top of the box to act as a sighting device: if you could see straight through the tube, you were on camera.

Needless to say, conditions aboard the balloon were very cramped, especially as it had to appear that there were only two people – David Attenborough and Don Cameron – on board. The other three had to sit on the side of the basket, their feet barely touching the floor.

(Above) The two balloons are inflated. (Below) Take-off at last (*RM/BBC Enterprises*)

All had parachutes on their backs, oxygen masks on their faces, and several layers of warm clothing, and it was something of a relief when the shooting was over and they began to descend again. But, as Martin Saunders relates, the landing was far from straightforward:

'I don't know much about ballooning, but one thing I soon learnt was that there is a delayed action to every manoeuvre. When the hot-air burner is switched on to get the balloon to rise, for example, there is a tremendous time-lag before anything happens, so you have to do everything a few seconds in advance. We were coming down in the middle of nowhere and the pilot was trying to find a suitable spot to land. He chose a field, but as far as I could see he was heading right for a barbed wire fence. We landed fair and square on top of that fence, the wire caught in the side of the basket, and the wind blew us along, tearing up a couple of fence posts. The pilot had turned on his burner, but it took a while for the added hot air to make us lighter and able to lift off again. Up we went, stopped, and had another go. The wind gusted at the last moment and hey presto we hit the fence a second time; this time it ripped along the fence and the basket tipped over. There we all were on top of each other, upside down, trying to make sure that our equipment wasn't damaged.'

Crash landing On a Scottish hillside, the team sort themselves out and pack up the balloon – with local help. David Attenborough is just glad it's all over (*RM/BBC Enterprises*)

When they eventually sorted themselves out, their first priority was to discover exactly where they were, get to a telephone and summon the ground crew to fetch them. From the air they had spotted a farmhouse nearby, so whilst the others were rescuing their various pieces of equipment, David Attenborough made his way down to it and knocked on the door. One would have thought that a farmer on a remote hillside would have been somewhat disconcerted at finding such a well-known figure on his doorstep, having materialised, apparently, from nowhere, but this one evinced little surprise. It turned out to be his daughter's birthday, and he pretended to her that he had arranged the visit as a special treat!

The stratosphere was the limit as far as human cameramen were concerned, but Adrian Warren and David Attenbrough wanted film from an even more distant vantage point – outer space. There are of course plenty of cameras out there anyway, beaming back pictures from satellites stationed permanently in orbit, and Adrian was able to obtain a time-lapse sequence which showed how the Earth's weather had developed over a 15-day period. One frame had been exposed every half-hour over that time through a special infra-red filter, and the film demonstrated clearly how a pair of hurricanes had built up off the West Coast of Africa, travelled across the Atlantic Ocean and dispersed, and how their remnants had ended up over Great Britain. As Adrian Warren admitted, 'It's difficult to get people excited about the weather', but this particular sequence portrayed the atmosphere as a living system, giving the view a space traveller might have if he glanced out of his window.

The film was, unfortunately, a black-and-white one. This was quite sufficient for the clouds, which were only different shades of grey anyway, but the Earth itself – the blues of the oceans, the greens and browns of the land masses – would have to be coloured artificially somehow, and the outlines of the continental land masses would have to be emphasised. Without a certain degree of exaggeration, the land would have been indistinguishable from the ocean. How could this be done, short of hand-colouring the film itself? The answer lay with graphic designer Margaret Perry, who had been using a three-dimensional model globe for several key sequences throughout the series, including the closing credits. This large resin replica – three feet in diameter – was minutely detailed, and had been hand-painted in realistic colours. By taking a still photograph of this and superimposing on it the successive frames of the clouds film, Margaret Perry was able to obtain an animated sequence. The outlines of the continents on the globe were scrupulously matched with the outlines on the film, so that the final result was completely accurate and startlingly dramatic.

The model globe and its recurrent use throughout the series was the last vestige of Richard Brock's original conception of a 'martian's eye-view' of the world. It became the instantly recognisable logo for *The Living Planet*, a largely blue ball covered in wisps of cloud, and floating in complete blackness. At the start of each programme, the camera would zoom in on it, and the globe was also a handy vehicle for transporting the viewer from one location to the next. But setting it all up was not quite as simple as it looked, as Margaret Perry explains:

'The major complication was that we needed to be able to represent a constantly changing cloudscape. The clouds couldn't just be painted over the top of the globe because they would have had to follow the contours and that would have looked silly: and besides we wouldn't have been able to make them move independently of the Earth itself. Somehow, we had to have a separate layer of cloud through which the details of the globe could be seen. For this, we bought another globe which was exactly the same size but coloured

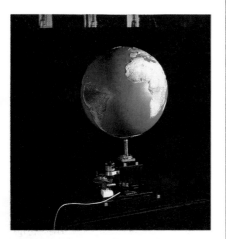

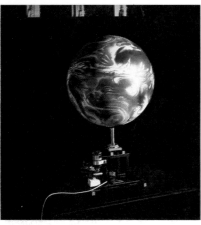

Margaret Perry and the globes The bottom one represented the clouds, and was superimposed on the topographical one above (*BBC Bristol*)

black. The cloud shapes were spray-painted on to it, using NASA satellite film as a guide. First of all, we filmed the Earth globe in what is called "stop-frame" – exposing a frame, moving the globe, exposing another frame, and so on – so that we got an animated sequence of the model apparently turning on its axis. Then we ran the film back and used it again to shoot the cloud globe in stop-frame as well, thus obtaining a double-exposure of one superimposed on the other. For the cloud shots the camera was moved fractionally nearer to give the impression that the clouds were actually wrapped round the Earth.

'Stop-frame is a pretty laborious process: in this case, we were exposing 24 frames per second of completed film, which means that one minute of film required nearly 1500 separate moves. For projects like this I am really an art director rather than a designer, because I have to work out the "plot" of the sequence with the programme's producer, and then devise a story board, which is a sort of pictorial script with a series of rough sketches on it mapping out each move. For the more complicated animations we were able to make use of computers. In the programme on mountains and volcanoes, for example, David Attenborough wanted to show how the continental land masses had drifted over the Earth's surface during the course of many millions of years. Cambridge University have a computer programme which can plot what the world looked like at any given moment in pre-history, and depict that on a screen from any angle that is required. By using a series of successive print-outs from this – 12 for every second of film – we were able to create an animated sequence which crammed several geological ages into less than a minute.

'The most daunting story board that I had to work out was for the programme "The open ocean". Richard Brock wanted to depict the view you would have from a submarine travelling across the floor of the Pacific Ocean. Filming this on location was right out of the question, because not only were the distances involved far too great, but at its deepest point – the Mariana Trench – the floor is seven miles down, and no cameraman could operate at that depth. So we had to get Oxford Scientific Films to build us a scale model instead. An American researcher provided us with a detailed itinerary of the underwater mountains and sand dunes, the textures of the rocks and the other key features of the route, and Richard translated it all into simpler terms for me. I made up a story board and went to consult with Oxford Scientific, who built a wonderful model and filmed it using their special "snorkel" camera, which is capable of tracking down and across replica landscapes. The whole room was filled with smoke to reproduce the murky underwater atmosphere, and after five days of shooting I was glad to get out into the fresh air!'

THE FINISHED PRODUCT
Organising, editing and sound

Cans of film, reels of tape, research reports, revised scripts, inflatable dinghies, thermal vests, invoices, airline tickets, lengths of rope, expenses claims: all these and more rained down upon the heads of those in the *Living Planet* offices as soon as filming began in earnest. Increasingly, it became a kind of clearing house where producers, assistant producers and cameramen might only meet each other on a few occasions during a whole year. There was a seemingly endless series of long-distance telephone calls to make or receive. Even the most carefully researched and painstakingly planned trip can run into unforeseen troubles through illness, accident, bad weather or the whims of the animal concerned, and it was usually up to Andrew Buchanan and the office staff to provide help and encouragement in the face of potential disaster.

Amid this welter of activity it would have been all too easy for the structure of the series itself to have started falling apart. After all, no one programme was being made in chronological order, and many trips were producing material for several programmes at a time. It was vital that someone should stay detached enough to have an overall view of how the whole enterprise was shaping, a role which fell naturally enough to the executive producer. Richard Brock had two programmes of his own to make, but he had to know everyone else's business as well:

'Although our three offices are next door to each other, producers tend to get so wrapped up in their own affairs that they don't consult one another very much. They just get on with what they have to do. I have to act as a kind of central intelligence, even going to the point of putting people in neighbouring offices in touch to make sure that they don't both go to the same country to try and film the same piece of behaviour. David Attenborough has the same sort of overview, but, because he spent the whole of one year solely writing the scripts, he was not always able to keep up with the filming. I had particularly chosen Adrian Warren as my assistant, because he was experienced enough to get on with the making of his two programmes without needing much help from me. My own programmes, on oceans and rivers, took up a certain amount of time, but left me with the breathing space to keep track of everyone else. I would need to know where each expedition was going and what it hoped to film to make sure that everything was meshing together properly. Then, when the trip was over, I would see all the rushes before the editor got to work on them, and be able to give a fresh – almost an outsider's – opinion on them.'

As the stacks of film mounted higher, the money in the series' coffers sank lower. There were 11 full-time members of the production staff to be paid, plus 2 editors, 2 BBC sound crews who were more or less full-time, and at least 40 other freelance cameramen in various parts of the world. Crews filmed in over 60 countries, and each member had to be transported, fed and housed – even, in some cases, clothed as well. On top of all this came the special apparatus, such as hot-air balloons and deep-sea submersibles, most of which had to be hired and none of which was cheap. Among Andrew Buchanan's many manifestations as unit manager was that of hawk-eyed keeper of the budget:

'The actual decisions about how the money is spent are taken by the producers, and my job is to keep track of what is happening and ring the alarm bells if either a trip is going to be too expensive or somebody is going to run out of money. Recently, for instance, Adrian Warren wanted to film some moths in slow motion which made it necessary to use a special camera which ran at 2000 frames a second. He asked me to look into the possibilities, and I soon discovered that the cost of ten seconds of film at this rate is quite horrendous, involving extra electricians, a generator and the camera itself which has to come all the way from London. So I had to ask Adrian if this particular sequence was absolutely necessary, and he tried to think of another way of doing it. Individual trips or filming sessions such as this will be costed out carefully, but the producers rely on me to keep track of the overall financial situation because I see all the bills as they come in.

'The trouble is that there are so many things that just can't be quantified. It's not as if we were making parts for a machine. For example, a producer may calculate that a cameraman should spend four days in a location in order to obtain a piece of film. Then, after the four days are up, he finds that the right animal hasn't appeared or the weather has been appalling, and he has to take the decision as to whether he should give the whole thing up or keep trying. This will be based on how important that sequence is to his programme, and the result is that we have to weigh up each individual project on its own merits. I would never dream of interfering with the ideas that go into the programmes themselves, but I do try to spot any logistical problems. There was a plan to send a cameraman out to Nicaragua, and I set about enquiring into the political situation there. It transpired that an American film-maker has been shot in Nicaragua six weeks previously, and our man very wisely declined to go.

'To put it simply, the money for the series is split into three lumps, one for each financial year. It is divided as equally as possible, with allowances made for rising costs and the other results of inflation over the whole period. Each programme is then allocated a serial number by which it can be identified in the accounts computer, and as invoices and so on arrive they are debited against the programme involved. When, for instance, a bill comes in from a freelance cameraman, I first of all check with the producer that that particular piece of work had actually been commissioned and carried out, and then I pass it on to the BBC's finance office. Many things go direct to the finance office before I know about them, so in order to keep myself abreast of the state of the budget I run through the accounts once every fortnight, using a computer print-out of the ledger sheets.

'Each invoice is attributed to a particular programme, and has the programme's computer number marked down against it. But it will also have to be defined as a type of expenditure – is it an artist's fee, or film stock, or overseas expenses, or the hiring of facilities, or whatever? The basic division is between resources and cash. Resources tend to be the things which the BBC already has on its books, such as camera equipment, editing equipment, telecine equipment, and the offices and studios themselves. These are all BBC property and there to be used, so of course we don't have to pay for them directly. Likewise all the Corporation staff who work on the series – editors, producers, camera crews and so on – are on the payroll and so their wages don't have to come out of our budget. Cash, on the other hand, covers all the extras, and this is where the £1.5 million goes to: air fares around the world, hotel bookings, freelance fees, helicopter hire charges, porters' wages, daily expenses – the list is endless, but every single penny has to be accounted for by placing it under the correct category on the computer. In reality, of course, it is mostly the public's money, because they pay the licence fees, so it is only right and proper that we should be careful about what we spend.'

The rate at which the money flows out is by no means constant. The bulk of the expensive location filming was done during the first two years of the project, with more than 40 trips having been completed by the end of 1981. The last 18 months were mostly taken up with editing the results and turning them into completed programmes ready for transmission. Over the entire period, two thirds of a million feet of film rushes arrived at the *Living Planet* cutting rooms in Bristol: that is, enough to stretch the 120 miles from Bristol to London – and back again if you include the negative! The film arrived from all corners of the Earth, which in itself was quite a triumph of organisation. If the cameraman happened to be near a direct air route to London, then the exposed film would be put on a plane as soon as possible. But if he were in some remote and inaccessible area, he would have no choice except to store up the cans and wait until he was back in touch with civilisation. Additional rolls of film will only increase the already considerable weight of equipment that he has to carry.

Film is precious stuff, and if it is lost or faulty the opportunity to re-shoot it is unlikely to come again. It is easily perishable, especially when unprocessed, and does not take kindly to extremes of heat or humidity, so the sooner it can be got back to Britain the better. In order to maintain an even standard of processing, all film for this series was sent to the same Rank laboratories, which are among the best equipped in the world. No matter where they were (with the possible exception of Hollywood), some means would have to be worked out for flying it all home. This was usually the job of the producer's assistant, who would send a telex or telephone message to the *Living Planet* office giving exact details of when and where it would be arriving. BBC Shipping would do the rest.

From the laboratories the rushes – the first positive prints of the film – were dispatched to Bristol (the negative was put in store with reverential care by a firm of 'negative cutters' until the time came for it to be assembled into the finished programme). Here, the first person to see them was often Beth Huntley:

'I would go down to the viewing theatre, watch them all and classify them in terms of subject matter. I had to make a list of what happened on each reel, shot by shot, and watch out for any technical faults. If the crew was still out on location they had to know as quickly as possible if there was, say, a scratch on the film which made it unusable, so that they could go out and shoot it again. The "rushes report" had to be sent out to them by any means possible – telex, letter, via someone they might be meeting – so that any failures could be replaced. People over here in the office sometimes find it difficult to realise how much store the film crews set by these reports: all they may have is a dozen lines of comment on perhaps six weeks' worth of work, and if you're too critical their morale can sink alarmingly, and they can be depressed for the rest of the trip.'

Reports are also sent from the laboratories themselves, where the technicians are less concerned about the professional feelings of the cameramen than the precise quality of the film. These reports are invariably terse and to the point and, if taken too seriously, can cause greater gloom than the more subjective views of the production staff. Martin Saunders, a man of vast and varied experience, has learned to live with such dampeners:

'It's bad for morale to have problems in a film. If you have to re-shoot a sequence because of some stupid technical fault like a scratch, you know in the back of your mind that you've already done it to the best of your ability, and it becomes very difficult to put the same impetus and effort into doing it the second time. Fortunately, it has proved to be the case that not a lot does go wrong, especially if you're careful. The only problem you really can't do anything about is scratching. The film goes through the camera, gets exposed and is then wound back into the magazine: if there is a tiny bit of dirt or grit on the rollers it could badly scratch the film as it passed over them. The only possible way you could check for this would be to take the film out again and check it in daylight, but of course that would ruin it anyway.

'Another thing to watch out for is called "hair in the gate"; 16 mm film is quite a small format to be working with, so if you get a little bit of dust or, as is more often the case, a piece of emulsion which has peeled off the film, and this lodges in the camera gate it will appear bigger on the screen than you would image by the time it has been blown up. With 8 mm film the result can be completely disastrous. So, while I am filming it is the job of the assistant cameraman to check the mechanical operation of the camera. After every take, if possible, he takes the lens off and inspects the front of the camera with a magnifying glass to see if there are any hairs there. Having done that he puts the lens back in, takes the magazine off and looks at the last piece of film to be exposed to make sure that it's not being scratched.'

It is a far cry from the jungles of Borneo or the ice floes of Antarctica to 19 Tyndalls Park Road, Bristol. At one extreme is the cameraman, who may be perched in a cramped hide waiting for a tiger, stretched out flat on the tundra filming caribou, or swimming among sharks in the Indian Ocean. At the other is the chief film editor Andrew Naylor, sitting for three years in semi-darkness in the same room, staring at a flickering image on the tiny screen in front of him:

'I started work on the series two-and-a-half years before transmission, although my assistant Sue Outlaw had already been hard at it for six months, viewing the rushes as they came in, logging the numbers printed down the edge of each roll of film and filing them away on shelves. A year later there was more than enough work for a second cutting room to start editing as well, and so I was joined by David Barrett who had been part of the *Life on Earth* team. Even then we were pushed to get the series completed on time.

'The film editor's art defies easy description. It's very much simpler to point out what is bad about the editing of a sequence than what is good for, unlike the cameraman whose work is displayed on the screen for all to see, the editor's work should for the most part not be noticed but, one hopes, appreciated at the end of the film. The essence of it lies in making a selection from the options offered by the material that is supplied to him and in assembling the selected shots in such a way as to produce a smooth and effective sequence. The sheer bulk of the material makes natural history film-making a much more laborious and instinctive process than, for example, film drama where normally each shot is scripted in advance and the editor can follow the script closely. Very few animals respond to direction, and it is not uncommon for a cameraman to shoot 25 times the amount of film needed for a particular sequence in order to obtain complete coverage of an unpredictable situation. The film editor's job is to create continuity of action from what can sometimes be chaos.

'The film comes into the cutting rooms in no particular order: there may be shots for different programmes on the same roll, in which case the roll is split and put into different boxes. Each programme has a different colour coding and its own area on the shelves, although we tend to rely a good deal on memory to tell us where a particular piece of film might be. The golden rule in a cutting room is to know what you've got and where it is. Over the weeks the boxes mount up. Once there is sufficient film amassed to start editing, the producer comes to me with his editing guides – the story of the film broken down into sequences which may be anything up to ten minutes in length. We then choose a sequence for which we have all the material, and as we view it he will give me an idea of the story he wants to tell and the feeling he wants to put over. He may express a preference for certain shots or point out something I need to know about how an animal behaves, but after that he leaves it to me. Most editors prefer to work alone once they know what is required of them: no matter how fond they may be of a producer, they won't want him breathing down their necks all the time! He simply has to rely on my judgement to pull together a sequence that works.

'The initial selection of shots from the rushes is a time-consuming job requiring a lot of hard graft and experience. It also calls for a good visual memory to recall whether, for example, the wide-angle shot of a male rhea moving right-to-left seven rolls previously will match the close-up I've just found. Was the background similar? Was the sun shining as brightly? Was the grass roughly the same length? Were those females as close? Only by careful and experienced judgement at this early stage can the next one – the editing of the shots into a smoothly flowing sequence – be achieved successfully. In an action sequence this smoothness may be obtained by timing the cuts from shot to shot in such a way that the action within the picture draws the viewer's attention away from the cuts. This is especially important when illustrating a process or pattern of behaviour. Sometimes, in order to capture a desired mood such as that, say, of a temperate forest, I may put together a series of unrelated shots using music, camera movement, movements within the picture or effects such as dissolves to achieve a smooth flow.

'There are usually problems, for few sequences go together perfectly. A vital couple of shots may be missing from a piece of animal behaviour, and I may have to get over this by cutting away to a shot of something else or intercutting two sequences or – as a last resort – dissolving between shots which won't cut together acceptably. In several instances in this series I had to flop the film over to change the direction in which the animals were moving. The rushes of the white-eared kob migrating across the Sudan, for example, were a shambles (through no fault of the cameraman, but simply because the animals were milling about all over the place), so to help the sequence make sense to the viewer I fixed on a main direction for the animals to be travelling in and flopped over several shots to maintain continuity in that direction. Then there were some rare footages which had to be included somehow, even if the actual quality of the film was not quite up to standard. Sometimes it is necessary to alter the film to suit a particular purpose. For instance, if a piece of action is too fast for the eye to appreciate then I can send it to a laboratory to have a copy made which is slowed down or has a frame frozen. The shots which Martin Saunders obtained of the narwhals jousting with their tusks are very rare, but they were taken from a very long distance and had to be blown up. This made them rather blurry and grainy, but it was considered worth it just to get that unique sequence.

'Most of what I have been talking about so far have been "mute" sequences, without recorded sound. There are also several "sync" sequences with David Attenborough's recorded voice to be fitted in. Most of these are specially shot for the programme, but some are duplicated from other films which may have come from our own libraries or be bought in from other libraries around the world. We may also use spare matter from other films, called "trims", and it can be quite a problem editing a new sequence when somebody else has already had the best shots. There is still more material to be assembled into the film, including title sequences, credits, shots of the globe and animated graphics showing weather patterns, sea currents, continental drift and so on. Somehow from all these different elements an assembly is made which may be as much as two or three times the required length. This gives the producer and me a certain flexibility when we come to judge the combined effect of the sequences and the way they relate to each other: it is sometimes difficult to predict their relative merits when they are seen in isolation.

'At this stage David Attenborough views the programme and offers his constructive criticisms. It is very valuable to have a completely fresh eye on something which the producer and I will already have seen a score of times. One way or another the length has to be reduced – sometimes it's the producer who winces as a very expensive or difficult scene bites the dust, and sometimes it's me if they decide to drop a sequence that I've sweated blood over for a week! But gradually the long and disjointed film starts to come alive as the unsuccessful sequences are removed and the troublesome areas ironed out. At the "rough-cut" stage, when it is still slightly over-length, David will have another look bearing his commentary in mind. Then the whole thing is "fine-cut" – that is, until the final adjustments are made to give it polish and get it to the correct length. This copy is then sent to the negative cutters, who cut and assemble the negative to match it precisely.'

As yet, the programme has very little sound on it. The sync sequences, with David Attenborough talking to the camera as he walks across a beach or stands perilously close to a Komodo dragon, are vital to the impact of the whole series, but account for only a very small percentage of the sound track. The bulk of it is built up from a wide variety of sources and remains, in the strictest sense, artificial. The flap of a snowy owl's wings, the roar of the ocean waves, the thunder of buffalo hooves, the crunching of an egg by a Gila monster, the noisy dismemberment of a seal by a polar bear – none of these was recorded at the same time as they were being filmed, for the simple reason that no sound recordist was present. And the reason for that was, once again, money. It is an expensive enough business sending a cameraman to a remote location for three or four weeks at a time in the hope that he will return with a few minutes of useable film. If a sound recordist were to accompany him, the cost would be doubled immediately, and the budget could not stand that. An additional obstacle lies in the fact that the cameraman is often shooting animals which are some distance away – too far for a microphone to pick up any consistent or precise sounds.

Such difficulties are almost insuperable, even with the sophisticated equipment available to a modern film crew, but David Attenborough is convinced that matters have changed for the better in the 30 years since he first started making natural history films:

'The curious thing is that in the old days we had *no sound at all*. Everything was shot mute and we had to make up the entire sound track. For a man walking through mud, for example, we always used to use a recording of a donkey chewing hay which we played at half-speed – scroonch, scroonch – and that served the purpose very well. And if we wanted to convey total silence, we played a recording of the Victoria Falls rather slowly. Then there were all the well-known tricks such as throwing telephone directories into the air to imitate the sound of birds taking off.'

The compiling of the sound track was a lengthy and laborious process, for 13 different tracks were recorded and then mixed into the final product. First of all the producer went through the cutting copy of the programme in considerable detail with one of the dubbing editors – Sue Outlaw or Peter Simpson – working out which sounds were required and how they were going to be obtained. The sounds themselves came from a wide variety of sources. Wherever possible, they had been recorded on location, out of sync but as extras to the filming. The bottom-most layer of the whole complex structure was the 'atmosphere' track – a background setting hard to define and usually conveyed through the use of an authentic recording. The atmosphere of the pampas, for example, will be different from that of a desert: the wind will sound different, as will the distant noises and of course the hum of animal life. On top of this came the sounds made by the various species being depicted on the screen – the courting cry of an albatross, the call of a howler monkey or the roar or a lion. There was no way of faking these either and if they had not been recorded during one of the filming trips they could usually be found in the Natural History Unit's huge sound library.

The more workaday noises, such as animals feeding or birds flying, usually had to be faked, using an ingenious range of special effects. For many of these, the editors relied on the peculiar talents of Beryl Mortimer, a freelance specialist in the manufacture of noises to order and on cue. Popularly known as the 'footsteps lady', she had carved out an enviable, if arcane, niche for herself in the film world and came to *The Living Planet* fresh from working on a James Bond movie. Footsteps were her stock-in-trade naturally enough, but her techniques went far beyond the classic routine with coconut shells. For the flapping of birds' wings she used a bunch of ties and gloves, and for the chomping of a polar bear eating a ringed seal she chewed a mouthful of celery rather loudly. On occasions, the production team had to go to far greater lengths to get exactly the right sounds on tape, as Andrew Buchanan recalls:

'Here's a story which graphically demonstrates how quickly a highly-organised recording session can turn into a nightmare. The dubbing theatre has to be booked well in advance, because it has to accommodate many other programmes as well as *The Living Planet*, and I have to make sure that everyone involved turns up at the right time and knows what is expected of them. In this instance, we were going to record one of David Attenborough's commentaries, make a final sound mix for the programme "The northern forests", and tape some sound effects for Richard Matthews' programme on grasslands, "Seas of grass". This last item was slightly complicated: Richard had already been out to the Sudan and had filmed the migration of the herds of white-eared kob and the way in which the tribesmen hunted them, but because of the remoteness of the location it had all been shot mute. What we now needed was a sound track with some fairly authentic Sudanese hunting cries on it, mingled with a lot of scurrying, puffing and panting, which could be dubbed over the top of the sequence. For this we had located and hired some students from Southern Sudan who were studying in London and who assured us that they could reproduce the right sorts of whoops and exhortations.

'First thing in the morning I checked that everybody had turned up. Obviously they are all responsible adults, but if someone is missing maybe they just need chasing up. David Attenborough was there, the recording engineer was there, the film was there and therefore they could begin doing the commentary for "Northern forests". I wandered off and did a bit more checking and then discovered to my horror that the Sudanese students hadn't turned up. One of them apparently had had to go for an interview, and the other's phone was out of order, and our production office was going crazy. And all the time the sound recordist was waiting. To cut a long story short, we had to rearrange the entire schedule and eventually at dusk only two Sudanese arrived. Richard Matthews said to me "Look, we haven't got quite enough people, so perhaps you'd like to join in", and off we all went to a park in Bristol to make this recording. The Sudanese taught us a few hunting cries on the way and there we all were in the pitch dark – the students, sound recordist, assistant producer, producer's assistant and me – crashing about in the undergrowth shouting out things like "Look out, it's over there, behind you!" or "I've got it! That one's mine!" There were various people jogging or taking their dogs for a walk who must have thought we were completely mad.'

The most important source of sound was of course David Attenborough's commentary, which overlays much of the rest of the sound track. Although it existed in a draft form in the scripts for each programme, it could only be written finally when the visual side of each programme had been developed to everybody's satisfaction, and a fine-cut version was available. David Attenborough has been writing commentaries for almost as long as he has been with the BBC but here, as in every other department of film-making, the techniques have changed a great deal over the years:

'I like to regard myself not just as a writer or a commentator but as a television programme maker. In my *Zoo Quest* days I was spending a hell of a lot of time in the cutting rooms virtually editing the films, and my view then was the same as it is now: you must always edit for picture and not for sound. The picture evokes the primary response from the viewer, so you have to cut the programme to make sure that the visual interest is maintained. After that it's up to the script writer – me, in this case – to write the commentary in such a way that it fits around the images. It is a sign of failure on my part to have to ring up the editor and ask him to lengthen a sequence so that I can have room for some extra explanatory sentences. Sometimes it occurs, but for me it is a failure, especially now that commentary writing has been made a much more comfortable business. Once the programme has been fine-cut, I am given a cassette of it which I sit at home and watch on my video player, stopping, starting and rewinding the action just as I want.'

Lastly, there was the music for the series. Both Richard Brock and David Attenborough were anxious to break away from the atmosphere of *Life on Earth* and employ an entirely different kind of theme and illustrative music. So they turned to the BBC's own Radiophonic Workshop (where the *Doctor Who* signature tune was invented) and asked for a pilot tape. The Workshop uses no conventional instruments, but creates all its own sounds on a variety of synthesisers and note-bending devices, and this technique had never been used on a natural history film before. So it was with a certain amount of trepidation that Elizabeth Parker, who had been asked to provide the pilot, set about her work:

'Basically, the pilot was to show the producers what sort of sounds I could produce and what sort of style and mood I could create. I was given a clip of film and worked pretty intensively for three weeks before taking it down to Bristol. I walked into the conference room which was full of people and I didn't know a soul: I was scared out of my wits! Fortunately they liked my tape and I got the job, although there was then a long delay before I had any programmes to compose for. There was no point in my composing anything before the film had been fine-cut, because the timing had to be accurate to a split-second. When at last a programme was completed – it was 'The baking deserts' – I looked it through with Andrew Neal and we pooled our ideas about where music was needed. I had to understand what it was he wanted; it was no good just pleasing myself because, apart from anything else, I knew very little about natural history. There was a great deal of experimenting at this early stage, with producers telling me what they did and did not like, and eventually a pattern began to emerge. One thing they clearly didn't like was the conventional synthesiser sound, which didn't go at all well with natural subjects, and so I had to soften the textures right down.

'For each programme I was given a cassette of the fine-cut, with a timetable showing how long each shot would last. I sat down in front of my video and watched it through, making a note of the exact points at which music was required and the amount of footage that it would have to cover. Then I took my notes and went home and later, usually after the children were in bed, I would sit down at the piano and compose a sketch for the music for one or two of the sequences, timing myself by the cassette. I would emerge with a bare outline which I could take into the studio next morning and start to flesh out with different sounds.

'Every note of music which you hear in the series was produced in my studio: no conventional instruments – symphony orchestras, bands or even any other musicians – were used at all. With our range of synthesisers and computers I was able to create virtually any type of sound I wanted electronically. I've got a big PVG synthesiser with a stock of 200 pre-set sounds which can be altered or re-shaped; it also has a computer attached to it through which I can feed in any other natural noise and it will be put on to the keyboard of the synthesiser. For instance I can sing a note into the computer which I can then play back on the keyboard either as a single note or as a chord. For other effects I used a string synthesiser which mimics the sound of violins, and a monophonic synthesiser, which mimics wood wind instruments and has a good reedy sound to it. I was also able to "bend" sounds by putting them through various electronic devices. In the programme about oceans, for example, I took a recording of waves and played around with it so that it could be used as music whilst remaining recognisably natural. That was the sort of balance I was after, leaving the listener not quite sure where the natural sound disappeared and the synthesised sound came in.

'It has been a fantastic experience to do a series like this, where everyone involved really cares about what they are doing. The production staff took a very close interest in the music, because every little piece of the series had to fit together properly if it was going to work as a whole. I have also learned something about natural history from them! When I began composing I was seeing animals in terms of black and white, and thought for instance that all those insects with their terrifying jaws and claws and poisons, crunching up their prey, were just nasty little creatures, and I wrote suitably sinister music for them. But the producers taught me that they are not nasty at all, and that each has its own part to play and life to live. I hope that my growing sympathy comes over on the sound track.'

Elizabeth Parker recorded her music on eight tracks, which then had to be mixed into a single track. When it reached the BBC studios it became only one of 13 tracks, made up of synchronised speech, voice-over commentary, sound effects and different atmospheres, which had taken about six weeks to put together. With the aid of cue sheets which showed the position of each item of sound in the 13 sound tracks, all of these were gradually amalgamated into one by the dubbing mixer in a highly complex process which involved hours of attentive listening. The producer of each programme, the dubbing editor and the editor sat in close attendance throughout, giving advice on the balance and accuracy of the sounds, and keeping sharp ears open for unwanted noises. During the mixing of the sound track of 'Seas of grass', the 'atmosphere' of the South American pampas was evoked by a recording made in the English countryside, and several quintessentially English sounds (including church bells) had to be firmly blotted out.

By the time the sound track was mixed to everybody's satisfaction, the completed negative of the film would have been assembled by the neg-cutters. It would then be sent straight to the Rank processing laboratories where a first print, called an 'answer print', would be produced. It should by now, of course, have been in its final, perfect and unalterable state, but there would still be details to linger over. Was the picture precisely in sync with the sound track? Was the colour balance correct throughout, so that the colour of the library footage exactly matched that of the newly shot material? After scrutinising every answer print in company with the programme's producer, the film editor travelled to the laboratory to discuss remaining problems with Rank's film grader, who made any final adjustments which were necessary. At last, the 'transmission' print was produced, and all that travelling, pondering, sweating, cursing, rejoicing and agonising was boiled down into a roll of film and a roll of soundtrack, ready to be shown to the world.

SOMETHING TO SELL

The six months before *The Living Planet* was due to go out for the first time on BBC1 were, as Richard Brock bluntly put it, 'very hectic'. They were hectic for the producers, who each had the finishing touches to put to their final programmes; they were hectic for the editors who, being perfectionists, were making improvements until the last minute; they were hectic for the dubbing mixers, who had to complete the sound tracks as soon as David Attenborough's commentary and the music had been recorded. The bottom of the budget barrel was in sight as well, and the last few filming trips had to be got out of the way as swiftly and as cheaply as possible. The final journey abroad did not take place until the December of 1983, when Andrew Neal, David Attenborough and a sound crew travelled to Jordan to shoot a sync sequence for 'New worlds'. The final location shooting of all – for the same programme at the Avebury Stone Circle in Wiltshire – was completed in the following January only a few days before the series was to begin its transmission run.

They were particularly hectic months for David Attenborough himself. Quite apart from completing the commentaries, recording them and giving close attention to the progress of the editing, he had a bestselling book to write. Judging by the phenomenal success of the book *Life on Earth*, which sold over three million copies in Britain in its first five years, *The Living Planet* could scarcely fail. Being an author, however, does not come easily to David Attenborough, who would much rather be out in the open air than hunched over a typewriter:

'I find writing extremely hard work, especially when I am having to do it at the same time as travelling and writing commentary scripts. If I came to the end of making the series and my publishers said "Right, now you can go away for six months and write the book", then I think I would quite enjoy the job, because I would be able to give a considered and leisurely view of the subject. But writing it on location in the evenings at the hotel after a hard day's shooting is frightful – particularly if you're in Venezuela and the chapter you're writing is about the Arctic Circle! There is also the problem of completing the book before I have written the final scripts for some of the programmes: although the television scripts and the book are separate matters, I like to keep their viewpoints consistent with each other.'

As the transmission date loomed nearer, Attenborough had another inescapable duty to perform – the giving of interviews. An apparently endless stream of journalists from newspapers, magazines, television and radio was clamouring for his attention, and he submitted to them with the good grace of a seasoned professional and the willingness of a man inexhaustibly fascinated with his subject. As the figurehead for the series it was clearly his job to do so:

'It is extremely flattering that people should want to know about your every movement, the reason why you blink your eyes in a certain way at a certain moment and all that. After all, your chance of doing another series will depend on how many people watch this one – the viewers are your bread and butter. You also have an obligation to make yourself available and explain yourself, particularly if you believe that what you are promoting is not just empty-headed and fatuous but an important contribution to the way people understand the world they live in. Inevitably, though, I find myself repeating myself. If I've been asked once I've been asked a thousand times: "Tell me, how does this new series differ from *Life on Earth?*" Of course you can't blame people for putting the question because it is a natural one to ask, but answering it did become fairly boring after a while!

'It was difficult not to feel harassed at this period as well. The last nine months of filming were a time of very high stress, and simply dealing with everything required by programme producers, film editors, publishers and interviewers gave me a sense of being driven and persecuted. No sooner would I get home from a foreign trip or a commentary recording session in Bristol than the phone would ring and someone would say: "I'm sorry to bother you but . . ." That level of pressure eased considerably as soon as the series had begun

transmission, and when it was all over I felt that I needed a change rather than a rest. At any rate, I have no immediate plans for another 12-part blockbuster.'

Richard Brock has, on the other hand, and is preparing a series on Man's relationship with nature, past, present and future. Meanwhile, he is making films for the well-established *Wildlife on One*. The rest of the team have gone their separate ways, too. Ned Kelly and Ian Calvert are involved in a geological and wildlife series about the Mississippi; Andrew Neal is the executive producer for the magazine programme *Nature*; Adrian Warren went back to Ecuador to make a film on the Waorani Indians and is now working with Jeffery Boswall on a three-part series to be called *Birds for All Seasons*; and Richard Matthews is making a *Natural World* programme on a national park in Brazil. Martin Saunders, Dicky Bird, Hugh Maynard and the rest of the BBC technicians have gone back to their life of variety and surprises, with Wembley one minute, and the Arctic the next. The mountains of paperwork have been filed away lovingly, though they may never be looked at again. The maps have been taken down from the walls, and the offices have been taken over by other producers making new programmes. But the making of *The Living Planet* is not over in one place – the film library, where the cataloguing of many miles of unused rushes is likely to take several years yet.

A legacy of cans The editing and sound team back in Bristol. (from front to back) Susanne Outlaw, Andrew Naylor, David Barrett, Nigel Kinnings and Peter Simpson (*AW*)

APPENDIX 1

Programmes in the series

Title	Abbreviation	Producer	Assistant Producer
The building of the Earth	BE	Ned Kelly	Ian Calvert
The frozen world	FW	Ned Kelly	Ian Calvert
The northern forests	NF	Ned Kelly	Ian Calvert
Jungle	J		Adrian Warren
Seas of grass	SG	Andrew Neal	Richard Matthews
The baking deserts	BD	Andrew Neal	Richard Matthews
The sky above	SA		Adrian Warren
Sweet fresh water	SFW	Richard Brock	Adrian Warren
The margins of the land	ML	Andrew Neal	Richard Matthews
Worlds apart	WA	Ned Kelly	Ian Calvert
The open ocean	OO	Richard Brock	Adrian Warren
New worlds	NW	Andrew Neal	Richard Matthews

APPENDIX 2

Overseas trips during the making of *The Living Planet*

This list is by no means exhaustive. It does not mention, for example, the numerous trips undertaken by foreign freelance cameramen or by freelance researchers. Nor, for reasons of length, does it mention every port of call on any particular trip.

Year	Date	Personnel	Destination(s)	Programme(s)
1979	2–18 October	Richard Brock	Canada/USA/ Norway	OO/SFW (recce)
	11–18 October	Hugh Miles	Norway	NF
1980	11 January–19 February	Richard Brock & Adrian Warren	USA/Venezuela /West Indies	SFW/J (recce)
	30 April–9 May	Richard Brock & Martin Saunders	Newfoundland/ USA (Chicago)	OO
	June	Hugh Miles	Norway/Finland	FW
	17 June–13 July	Stephen Bolwell	Hawaii	J
	29 June–17 August	Richard Brock, David Atten-borough & sound crew	Canada	OO
	November	Ned Kelly & David Attenborough	Iceland	BE
	11 December–17 January	Ned Kelly, David Atten-borough & sound crew	Antarctica/ Falkland Islands	BE/FW
1981	28 February–31 January	Richard Brock	USA/Canada	OO/SFW (recce)
	5–10 February	Ned Kelly	Norway	NF (recce)
	6 February–1 March	Andrew Neal	USA (New York, Washington)	BD (recce)
	9 February–7 March	Adrian Warren	USA	J (recce)
	5–12 March	Ned Kelly	Norway/Finland	NF (recce)
	17–23 March	Andrew Neal & film crew	USA (Florida)	NW
	22 March–18	Adrian Warren	South Africa	J (recce)

April			
3–11 April	Richard Brock	West Germany/ France	SFW (recce)
3 April–4 May	Ned Kelly	USA/Canada	FW/NF (recce)
10–26 April	Andrew Neal	South Africa/ Botswana	BD/SG (recce)
7–21 May	Hugh Miles	Norway	NF
8–22 May	Andrew Neal	Egypt/Israel	BD (recce)
11 May–8 June	Martin Saunders	USA/Canada	OO
18 May–29 June	Hugh Maynard & Jerry Gould	USA/Hawaii	BD/WA/OO
6–19 June	Adrian Warren	USA	J (recce)
15 June–30 July	Andrew Neal & film crew	USA (Los Angeles, Arizona)	BD
27 June–15 August	Roger Jackman	USA/Brunei ·	BD/J
28 June–25 July	Richard Matthews	Kenya/Sudan	SG (recce)
1–31 July	Ned Kelly & Hugh Miles	Canada	FW
3–24 July	Richard Brock, David Attenborough & sound crew	Finland/Switzerland/West Germany	SFW
18 July–22 August	Adrian Warren & film crew	Thailand/Malaysia/Philippines/Brunei	J
3–18 August	Ned Kelly & Roger Brown	Norway	FW
3–14 August	Martin Saunders	USA (California)	OO (recce)
22 August–12 October	Ned Kelly, David Attenborough & sound crew	Kenya/Seychelles/Aldabra	BE/SA/WA/ OO
2–4 September	Richard Matthews	West Germany	SG (recce)
18 September–4 October	Andrew Neal & sound crew	South Africa/ Botswana	BD/SA
1–7 October	Richard Brock & Peter Scoones	Norway	OO
1–18 October	Richard Matthews	USA (Colorado, Kansas)	SG
18–25 October	Andrew Neal & film crew	Israel	BD/OO
18 October–20 November	Andrew Buchanan	Algeria/Niger	BD (recce)
29 October–11 December	Richard Matthews & film crew	Kenya/Sudan	SG

	4–22 December	Andrew Neal, David Attenborough & film crew	South Africa	BD/ML/SG
	11–15 December	Ian Calvert	Finland/ Sweden	NF (recce)
1982	19 January–5 February	Andrew Neal, Andrew Buchanan, David Attenborough & sound crew	Algeria	BD
	20 January–3 February	Ian Calvert & Hugh Miles	Finland/ Sweden	BE/NF
	21 January–23 March	Richard Brock, Adrian Warren, David Attenborough & sound crew	USA/Surinam/ Peru/Brazil/ Ecuador/Bolivia	SFW/J/NW/ OO
	6–15 February	Ned Kelly	Nepal	BE (recce)
	14–27 February	Adrian Warren	Switzerland/ West Germany	SA (recce)
	25 February–4 March	Rodger Jackman	Israel	BD
	28 February–6 April	Richard Matthews	USA/Brazil/Bolivia/ Argentina	SG (recce)
	19 March–28 April	Ned Kelly, David Attenborough & sound crew	Nepal	BE
	19 April–18 May	Hugh Miles	Nepal	BE
	21 April–4 June	Andrew Neal, Adrian Warren, David Attenborough & sound crew	USA/Venezuela	NF/J/BD/SG/ ML/NW
	25 April–25 May	Ian Calvert	USA	NF (recce)
	7 May–1 June	Hugh Maynard	Kenya/Sudan	SG
	11–25 May	Richard Matthews	Israel	BD (recce)
	15 June–10 July	Richard Brock & Hugh Miles	Germany/ Yugoslavia	SFW
	12–17 July	Stephen Bolwell	USA (Indiana)	NF
	13–30 July	Hugh Miles	Canada	FW
	18 July–22 August	Ned Kelly, Andrew Neal, David Attenborough & sound crew	USA (Miami, Seattle)	BE/FW/NF/ML

	16 August–23 September	Ian Calvert	Hawaii/New Zealand/Australia/Indonesia	BE/WA/ML (recce)
	25 August–5 September	Adrain Warren, David Attenborough & sound crew	Kenya/South Africa	SG/SA
	27 August–10 October	Richard Matthews, Hugh Miles & Stephen Bolwell	Brazil	SG
	28 August–25 September	Andrew Neal & Hugh Maynard	Israel	BD
	14 September –29 October	Ned Kelly, David Attenborough & sound crew	Indonesia/Australia/New Zealand/Kiribati/Hawaii	BE/WA/ML
	4–8 October	Richard Brock & Hugh Maynard	Holland/West Germany	BE
	11 October–10 November	Adrian Warren & Neil Rettig	USA/Costa Rica	J
	31 October–30 November	Richard Brock	USA	SFW/OO (recce)
	1–17 November	Andrew Neal, Andrew Buchanan & sound crew	Niger	BD
1983	11–20 February	Richard Brock, David Attenborough & sound crew	Maldive Islands	OO
	13–20 March	Ned Kelly	Switzerland/France	BE/FW (recce)
	3 May–4 June	Adrian Warren	USA	SA (recce)
	30 June–16 July	Andrew Anderson	Canada	FW
	18 July–7 August	Andrew Neal, David Attenborough & sound crew	Malaysia	J/ML/NW
	7–17 August	Andrew Neal & Martin Saunders	USA/Canada	ML
	11–15 December	Andrew Neal, David Attenborough & sound crew	Jordan	NW

PICTURE CREDITS

INDEX